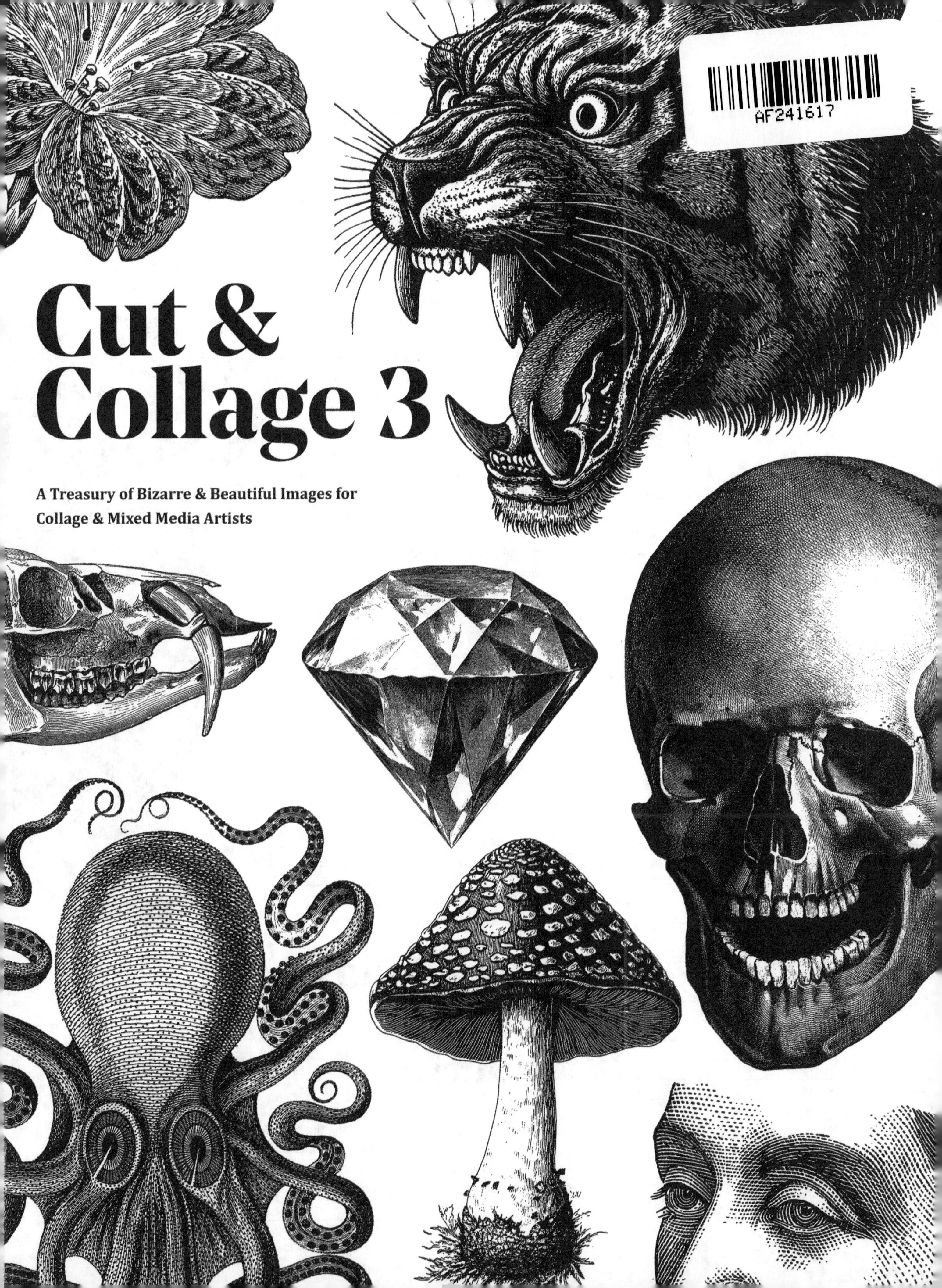

Cut &
Collage 3

**A Treasury of Bizarre & Beautiful Images for
Collage & Mixed Media Artists**

Introduction

Collage as an art form has long captivated creators and viewers alike. By recontextualising and combining disparate images, collage provides a unique avenue for artistic expression, allowing artists to construct new narratives ranging from the surreal to the sublime. It is a medium that bridges the worlds of realism and abstraction, merging elements from the familiar with the unexpected to evoke emotion, curiosity, and intrigue. In *Cut & Collage 3*, Vault Editions invites you to explore the boundless creative potential of collage, whether you're embarking on your first collage project or are an experienced artist looking to expand your repertoire.

This collection is crafted with a diverse subject matter to stimulate the imagination and offer endless possibilities. Inside, you'll find everything from detailed anatomical sketches that reveal the inner workings of the human body to delicate botanical illustrations that capture nature's intricacy. Alongside these, you'll discover enigmatic sea creatures, fantastical inventions, and mysterious statues, each image chosen for its visual impact and creative potential. Each subject has been meticulously restored to ensure high-quality reproduction, making this book an ideal resource for both physical and digital collage projects. Furthermore, *Cut & Collage 3* includes a downloadable PDF version, allowing you to print the images as often as you need without repurchasing. This approach supports continual experimentation and refinement, encouraging artists to revisit and reimagine each piece.

Perfect for artists, designers, art students, and enthusiasts, *Cut & Collage 3* appeals to anyone looking to infuse a vintage aesthetic into their work, experiment with surrealist compositions, or simply find joy in the meditative practice of cutting and arranging images. Whether you prefer working with paper or digital formats, this collection offers a wealth of material to bring your creative visions to life. Welcome to a new world of inspiration.

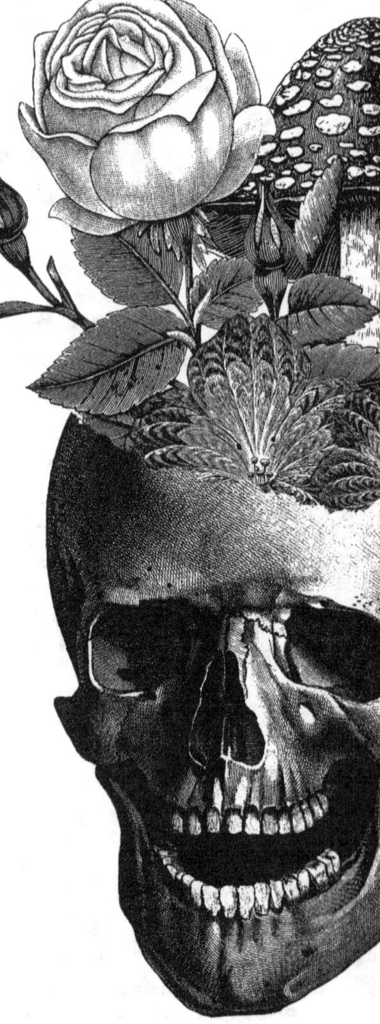

Table of Contents

Mammals	01
Birds	11
Snakes	15
Sea Life	17
Botanical Illustration	21
Anatomical Illustration	29
Sculpture	37
Angels	41
Inventions	43
Nautical Imagery	47
Clocks & Watches	51
Hearts	53
Insects	55
Monsters	61
Arms & Armour	69
Frames	79
Ornaments	85
Gems, Diamonds & Crystals	91
Men	93
Women	97
Architecture	103
Landscapes	111

Downloads + Collage Course

Downloading your files and accessing the course is simple. Go to the last page of this publication and follow the instructions to access the download page and online course.

Bibliographical Notes
This is a new work by Vault Editions Ltd

ISBN: 978-1-922966-52-0

Recommended Materials

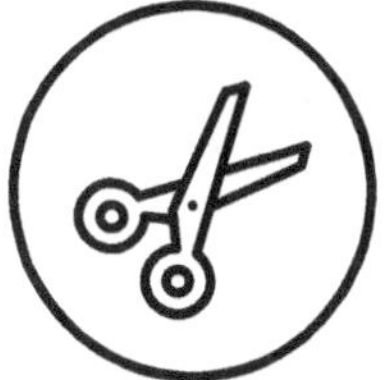

SCISSORS

SCALPEL

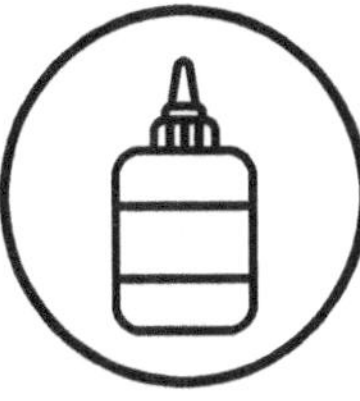

GLUE

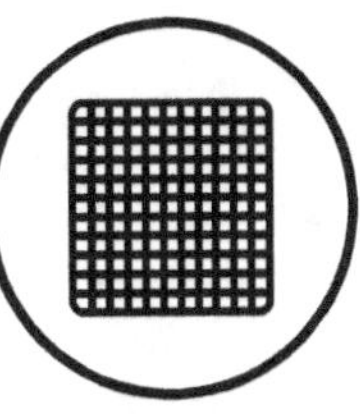

CUTTING MAT

HEAVY WEIGHT CARD

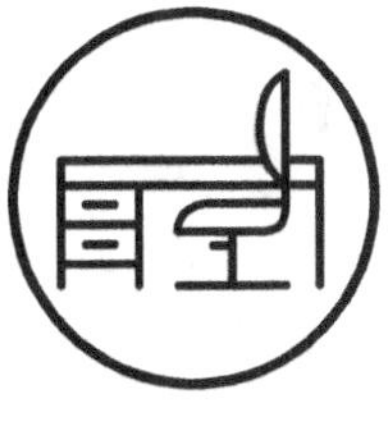

SAFE WORKSPACE

Collage is arguably one of the most experimental forms of visual art, and there are certainly no hard and fast rules on best practices. However, some essential tools and materials that will assist you in achieving the best results and will ensure the durability of your artwork.

Scissors:

We recommend a sharp pair of craft scissors to ensure that you avoid tearing the paper. It will also allow you to gain greater detail in every cut and will prevent micro-tearing and fraying edges which may occur with a lesser quality crafting product.

Glue:

The glue you are using should not contain too much moisture. An excess of moisture will lead to cockling of the paper which can leave an undesirable lumpy finish. It can also cause bleeding of the ink. We recommend either a high-quality glue stick for beginners, and spray adhesive for the more advanced.

Scalpel:

For extracting detailed elements from an image, we recommend using a sharp scalpel for best results. Ensure that you regularly change your blade to avoid fraying edge and micro-tears.

Cutting Mat:

A cutting mat is essential for anyone working with a scalpel. They're relatively inexpensive and can be purchased from any good arts and crafts store. They are a worthy investment to save your table from unwanted cut marks.

Substrates:

What surface should I apply my collage to? Again, there are no rules here, but we would recommend a heavy card of 350gsm or higher. If you intend to sell or gift your artwork, also consider using a paper size that will be compatible with standard frame sizes.

Workspace:

As you will be working with sharp tools, and generally making a bit of a mess, we recommend that you have an appropriate workspace with plenty of room to move. Ensure that your elbows are elevated above the table so that you have greater control of your movements when cutting to avoid slipping and any unwanted accidents. If you are working for long periods, consider investing in an ergonomic chair or standing desk to protect your back. These can be purchased from all good office supply stores. Many online reatilers will also have these available.

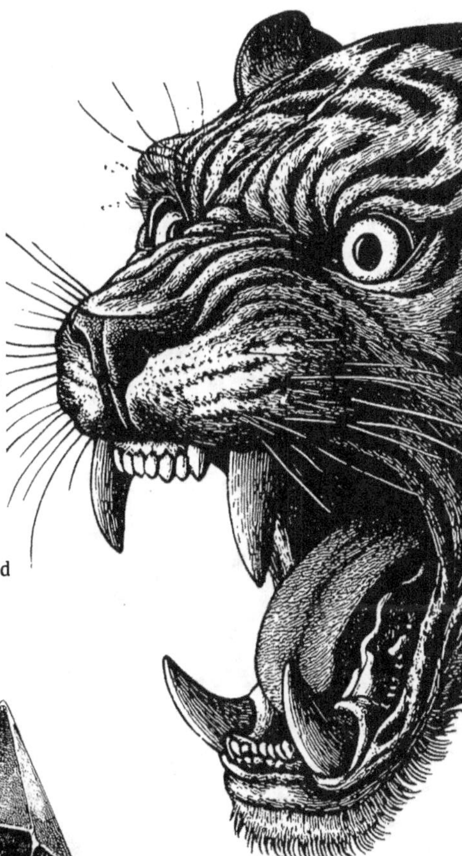

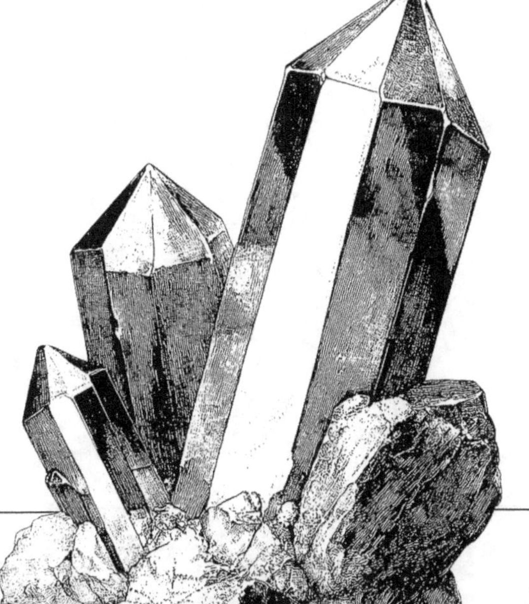

MAMMALS

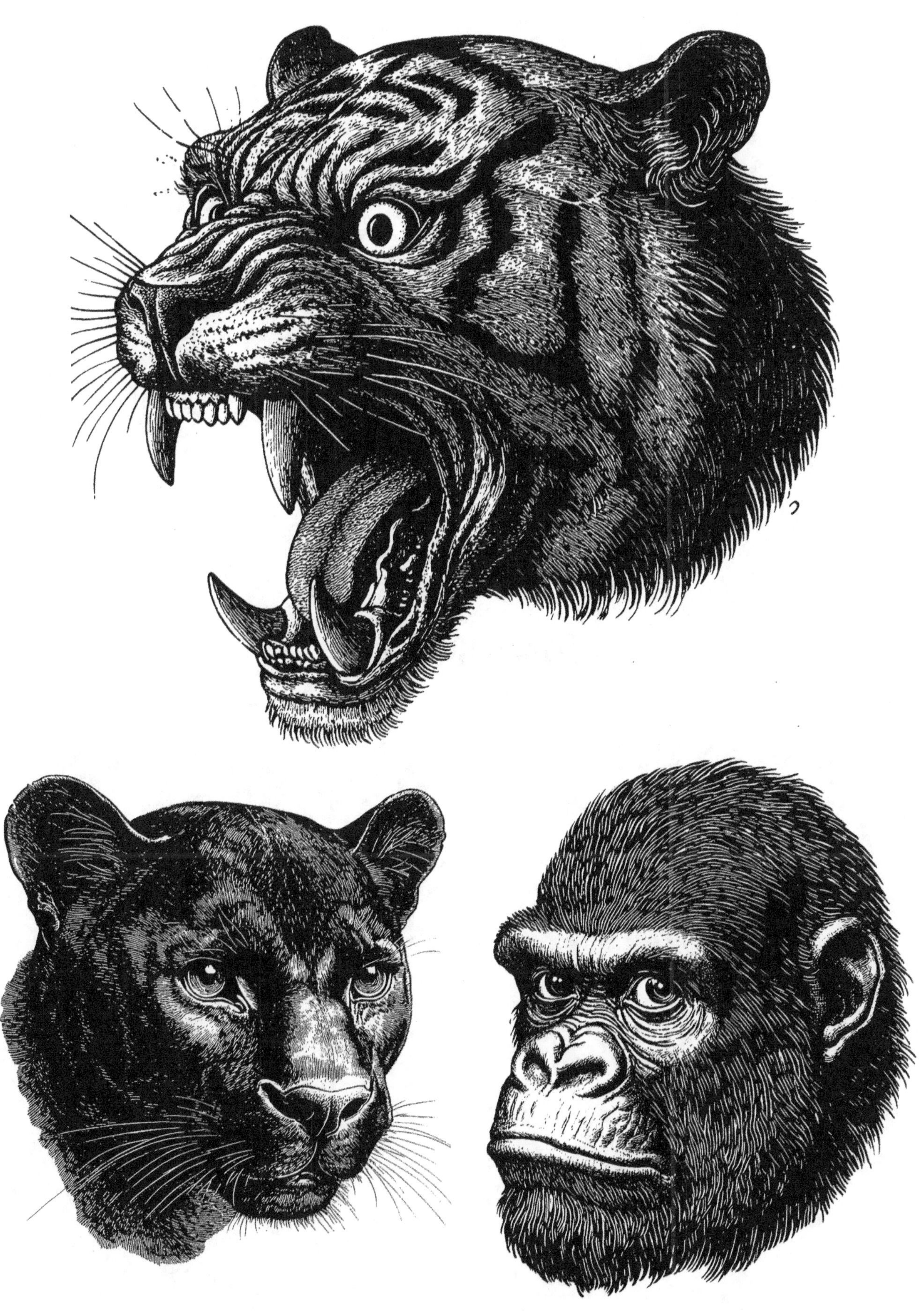

MAMMALS

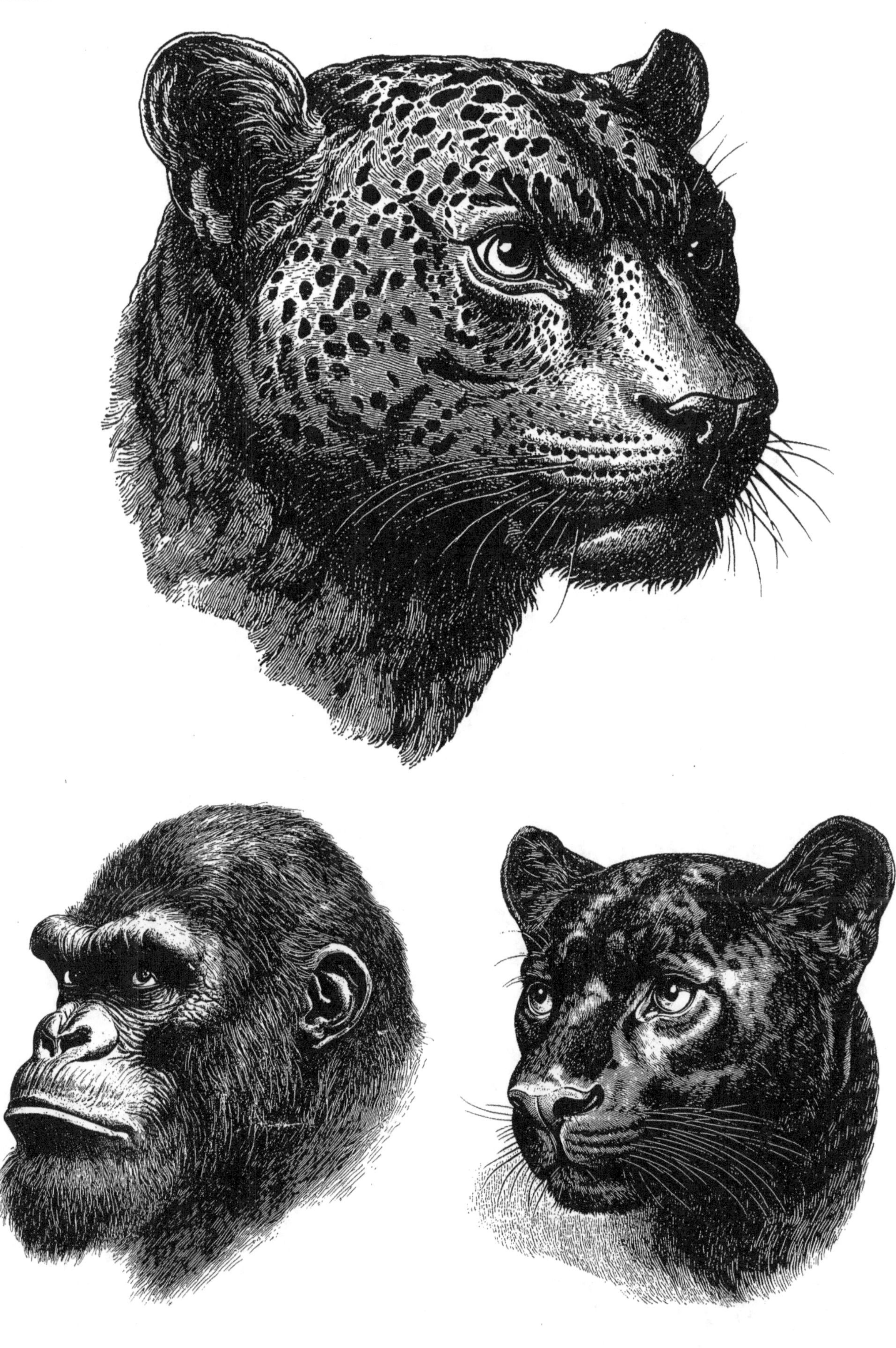

MAMMALS

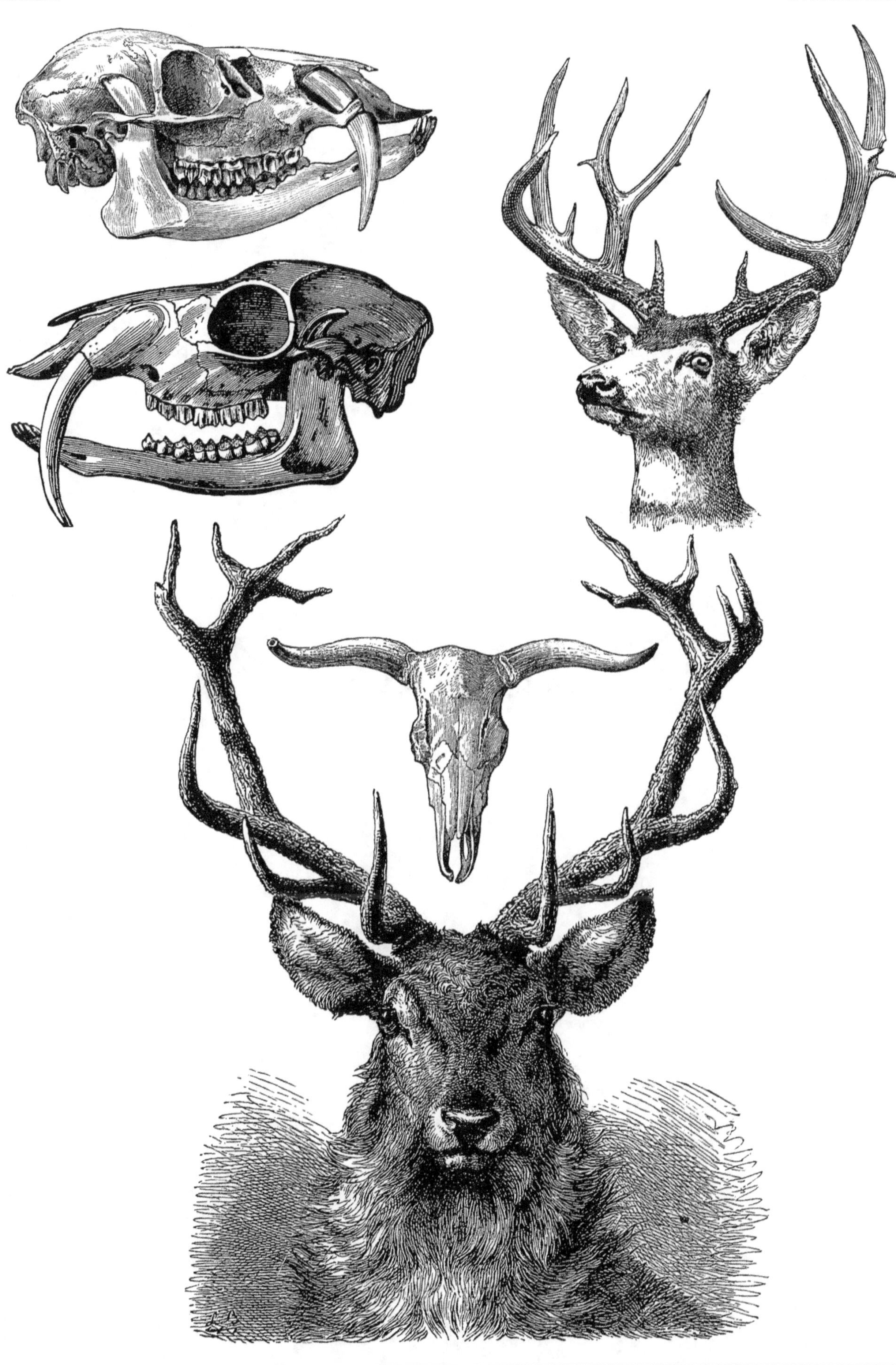

MAMMALS

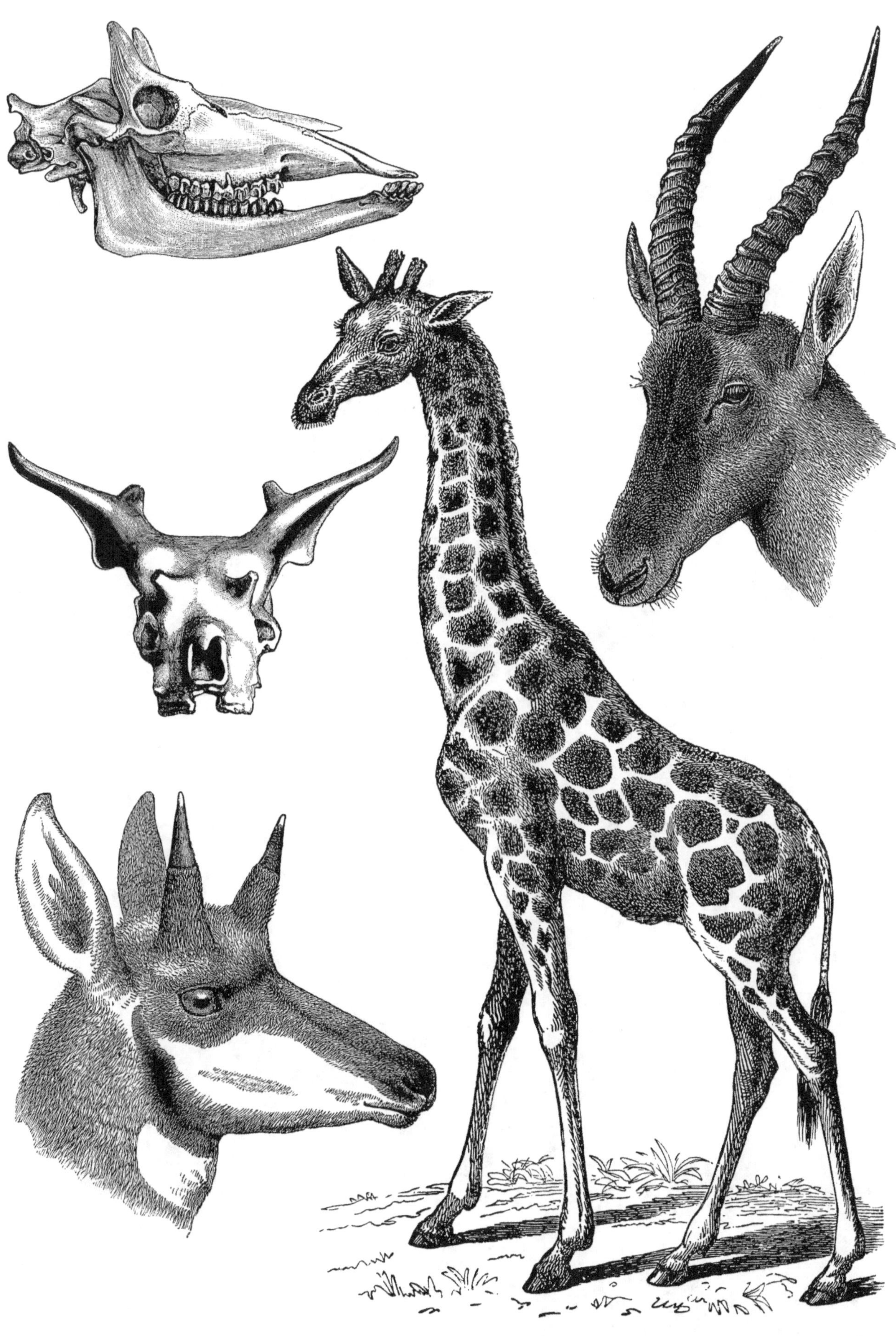

CUT & COLLAGE 3

MAMMALS

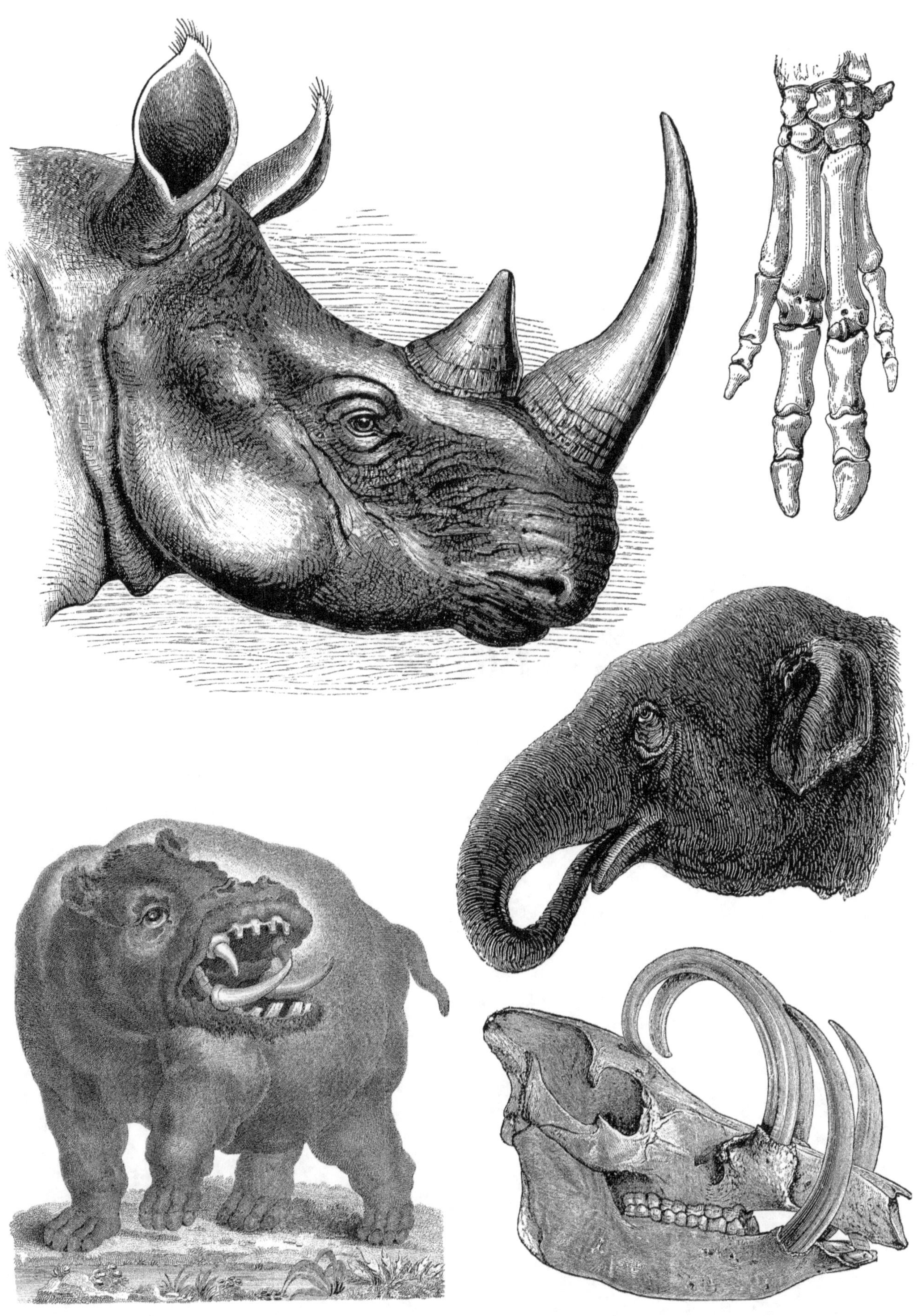

BIRDS

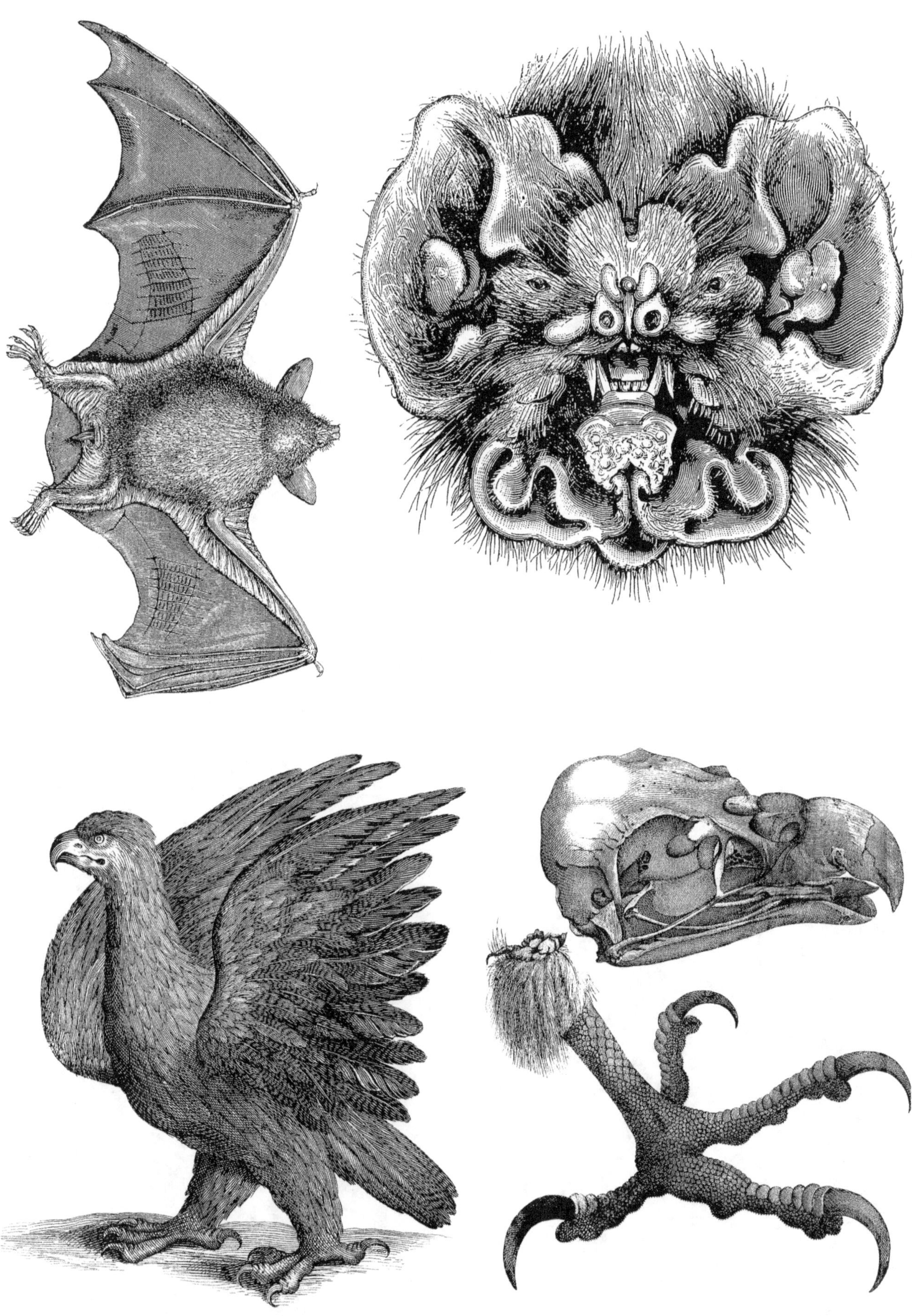

CUT & COLLAGE 3

BIRDS

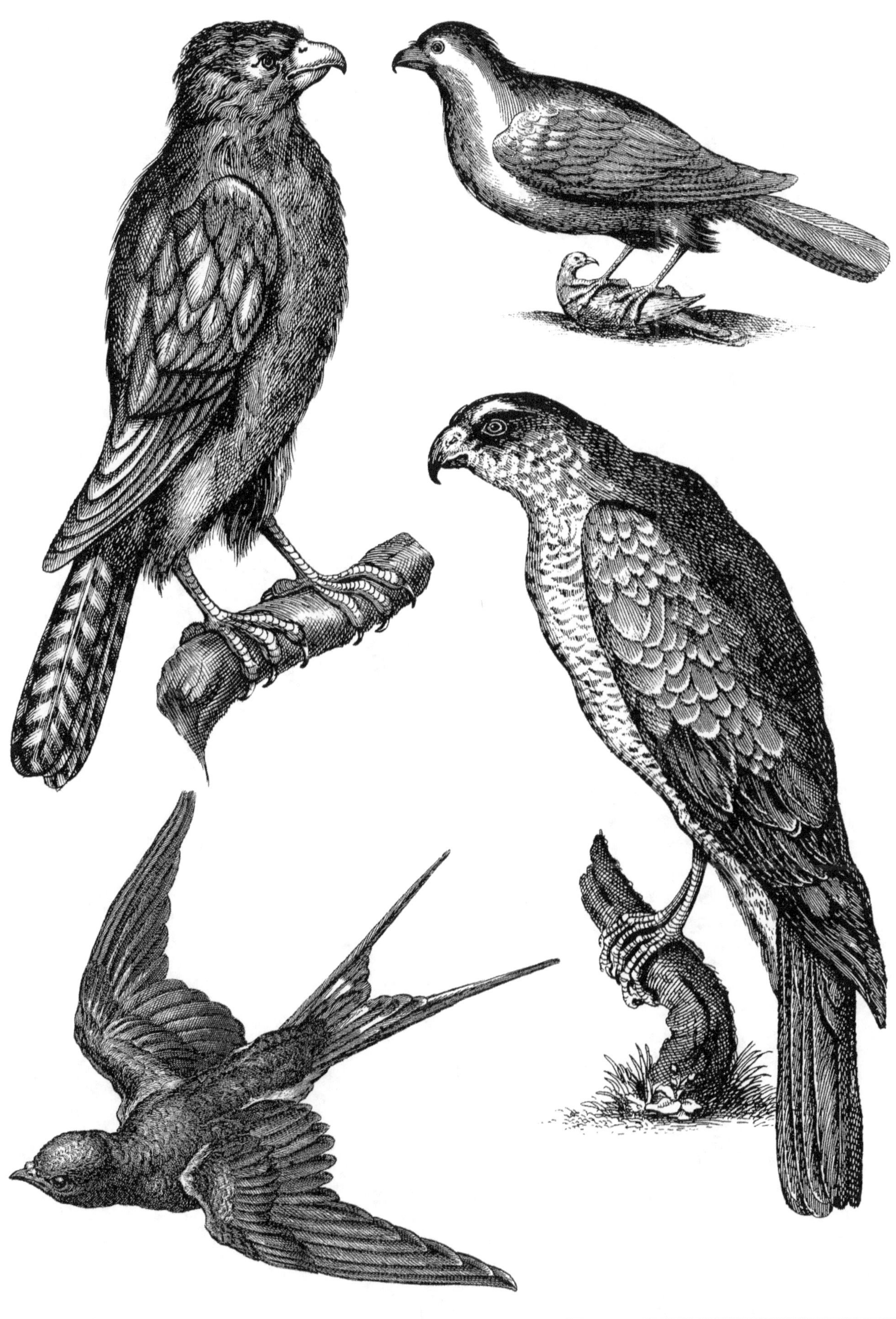

SNAKES

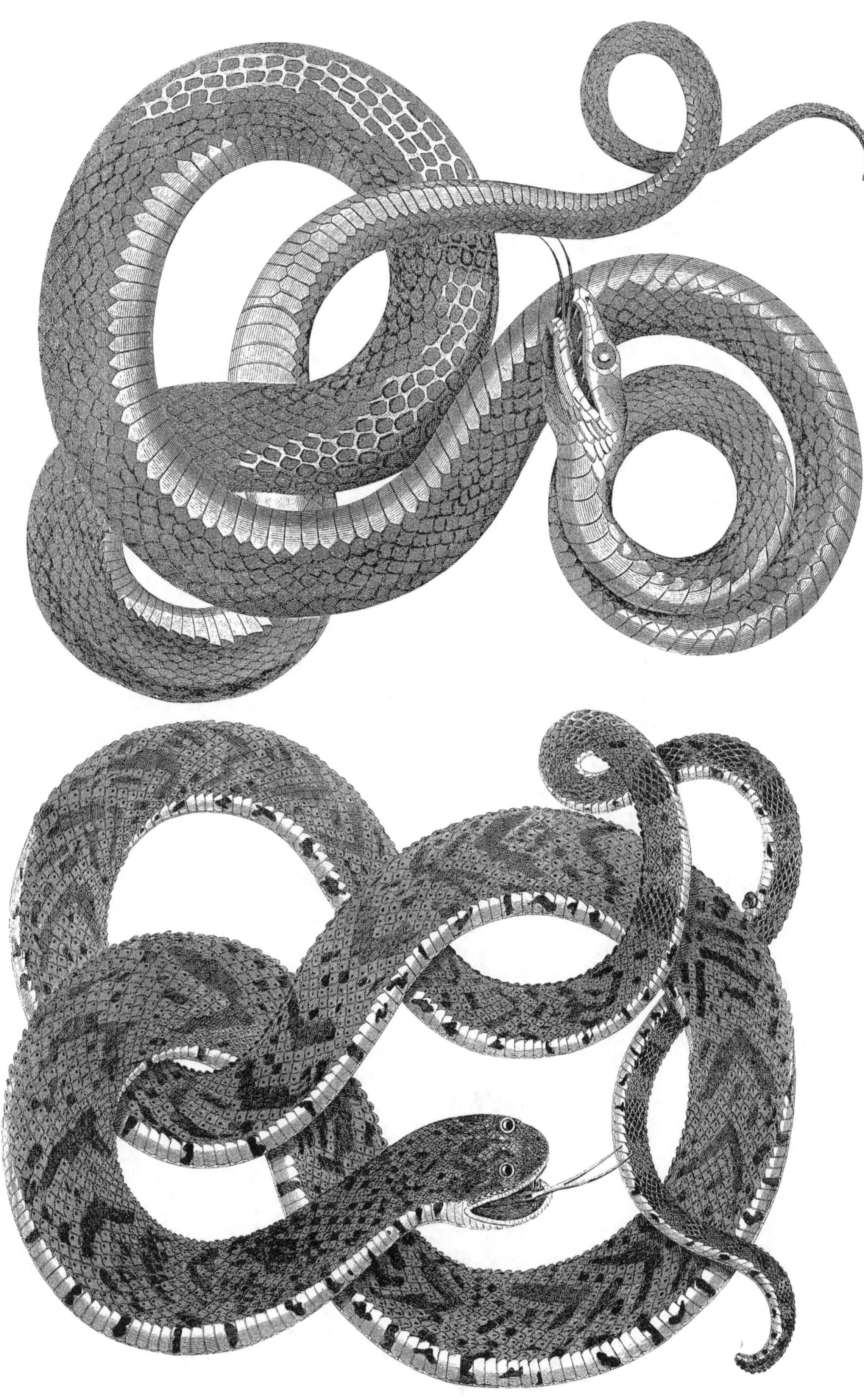

SEA LIFE

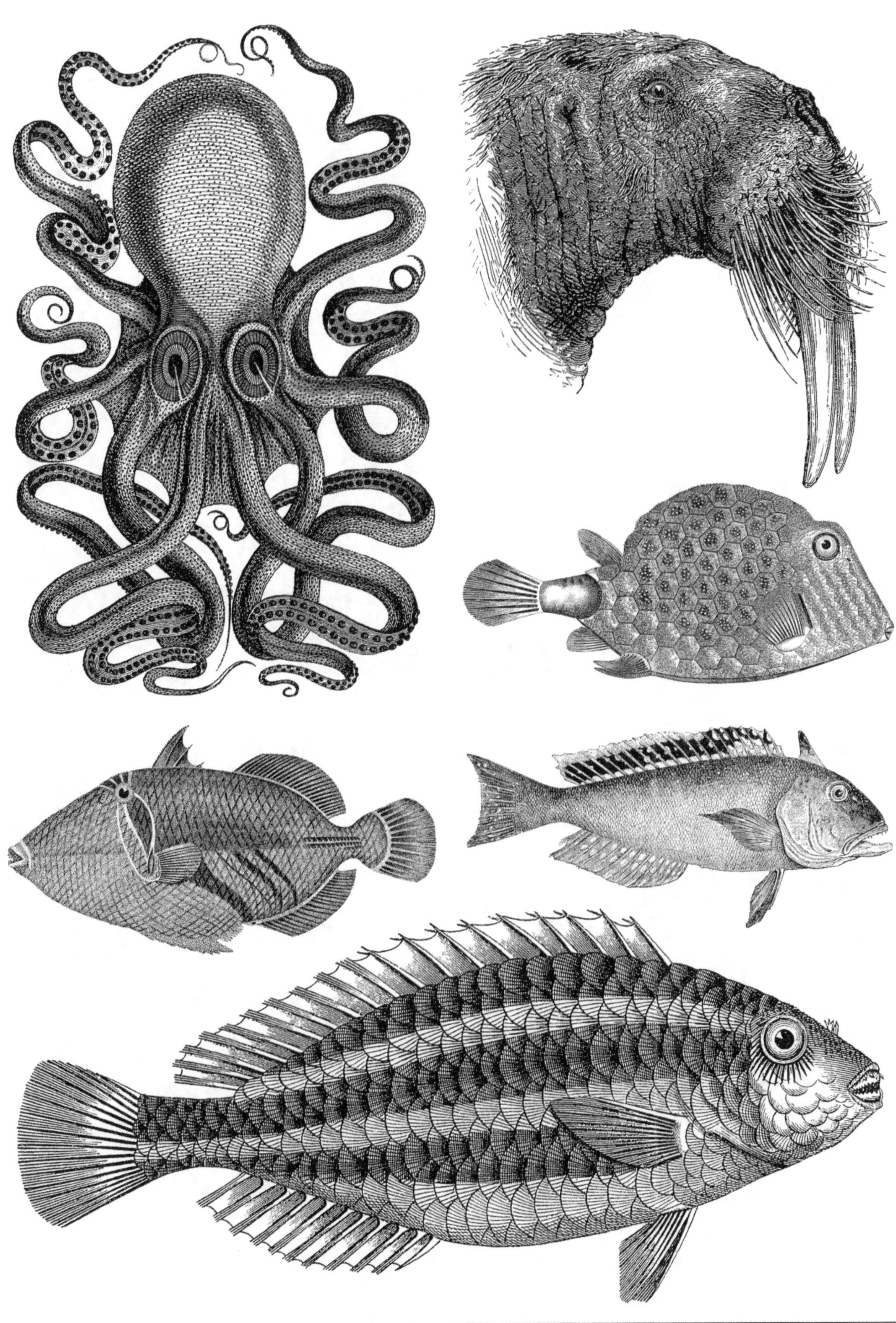

SEA LIFE

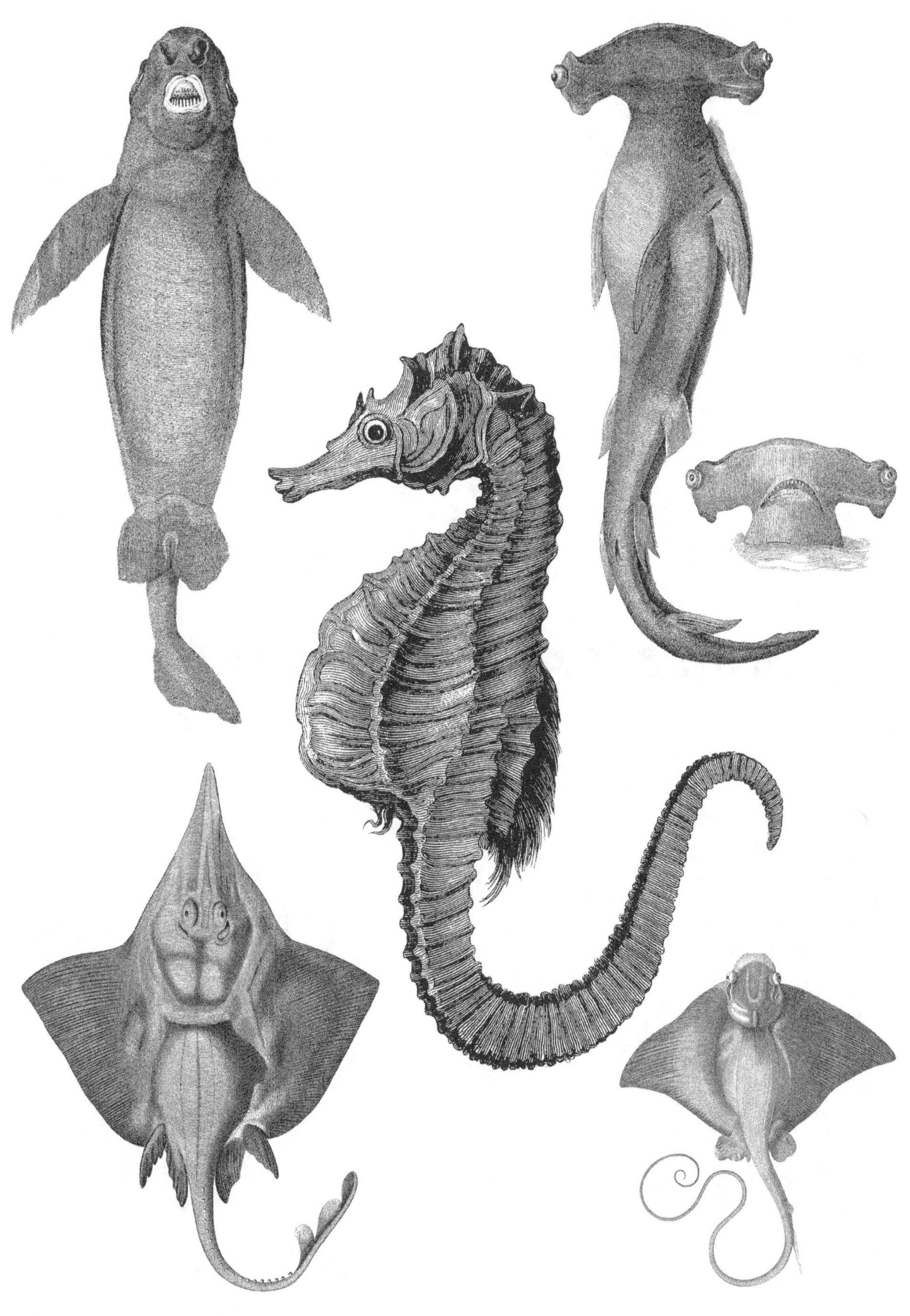

BOTANICAL ILLUSTRATION

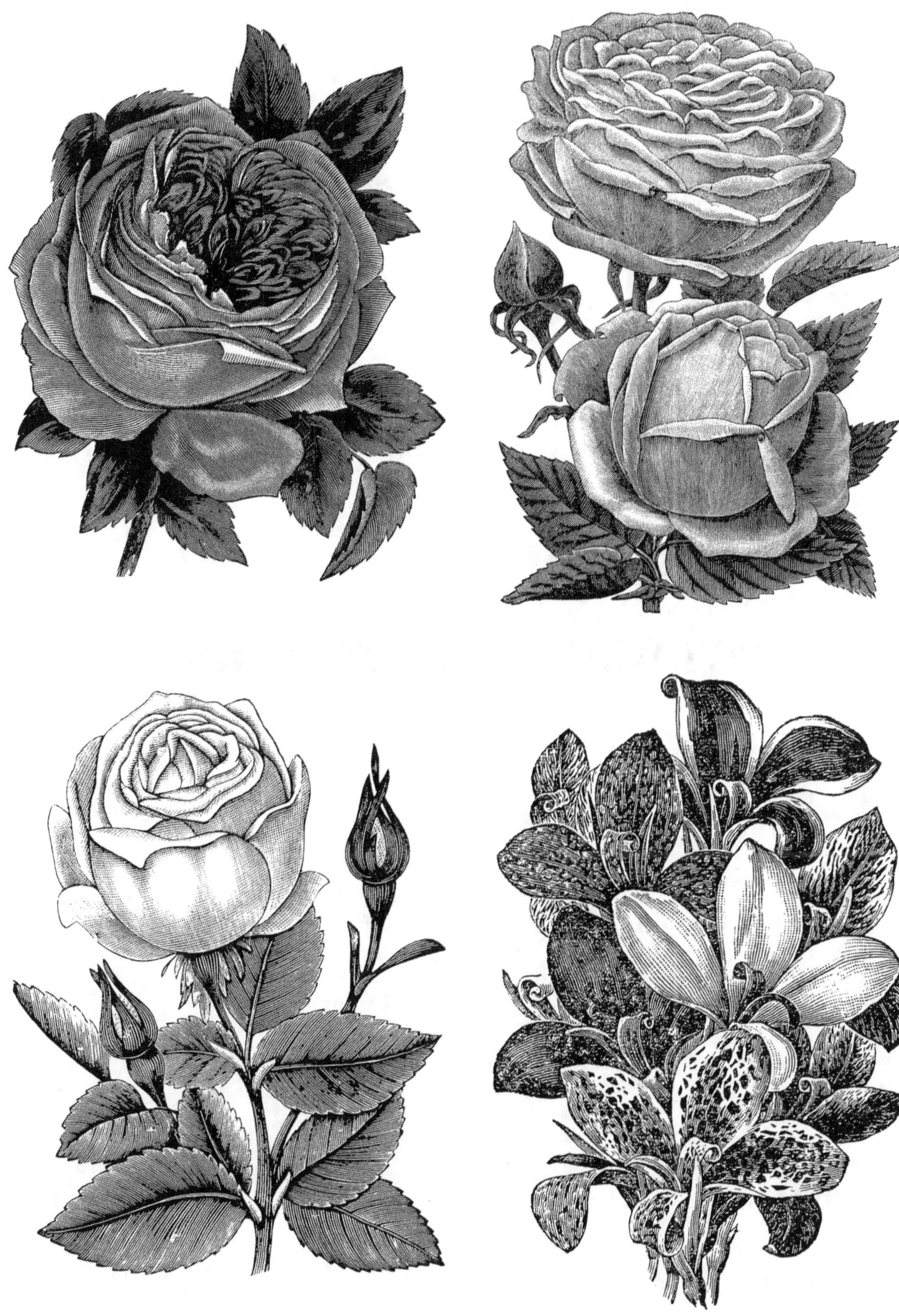

BOTANICAL ILLUSTRATION

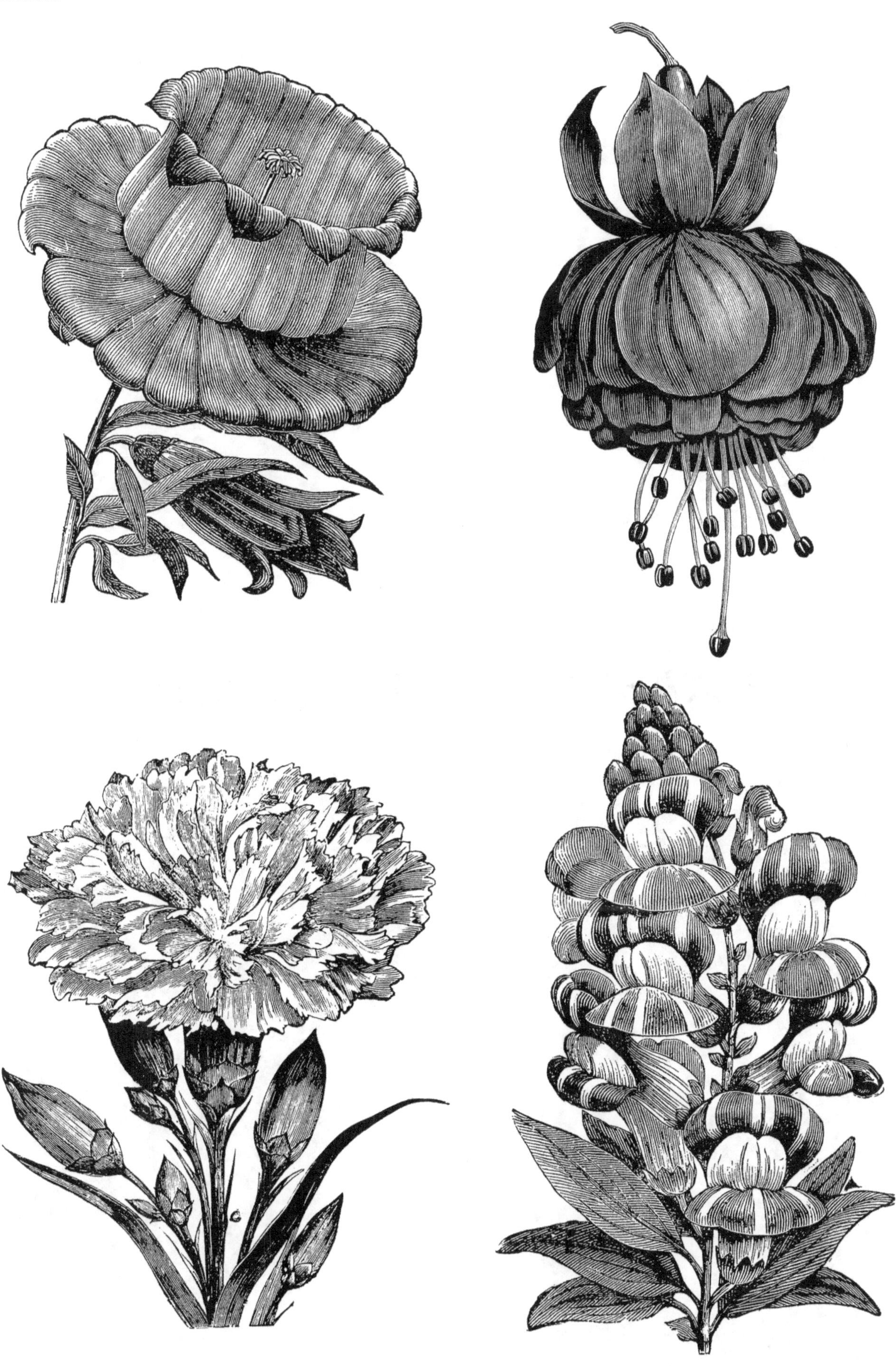

BOTANICAL ILLUSTRATION

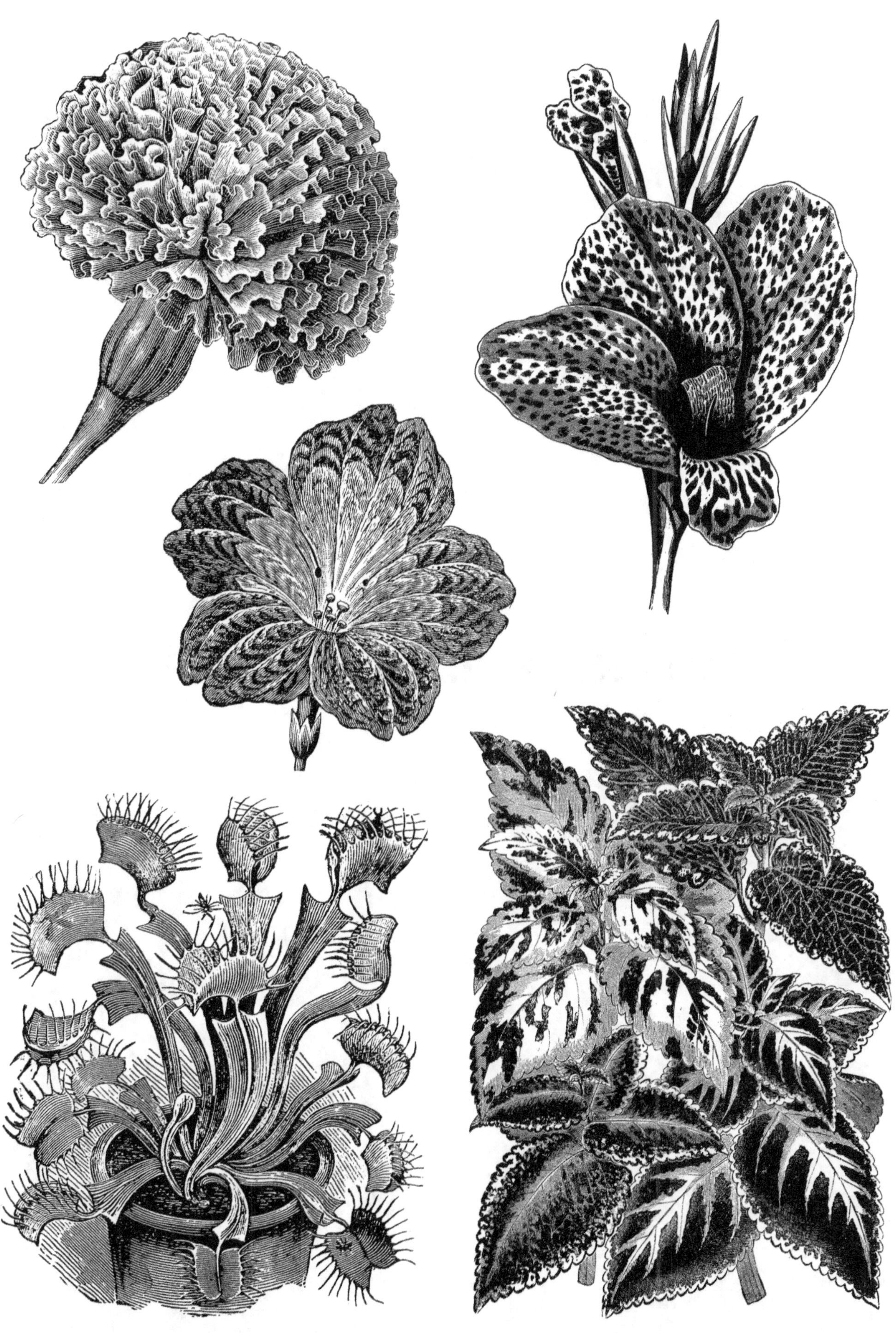

BOTANICAL ILLUSTRATION

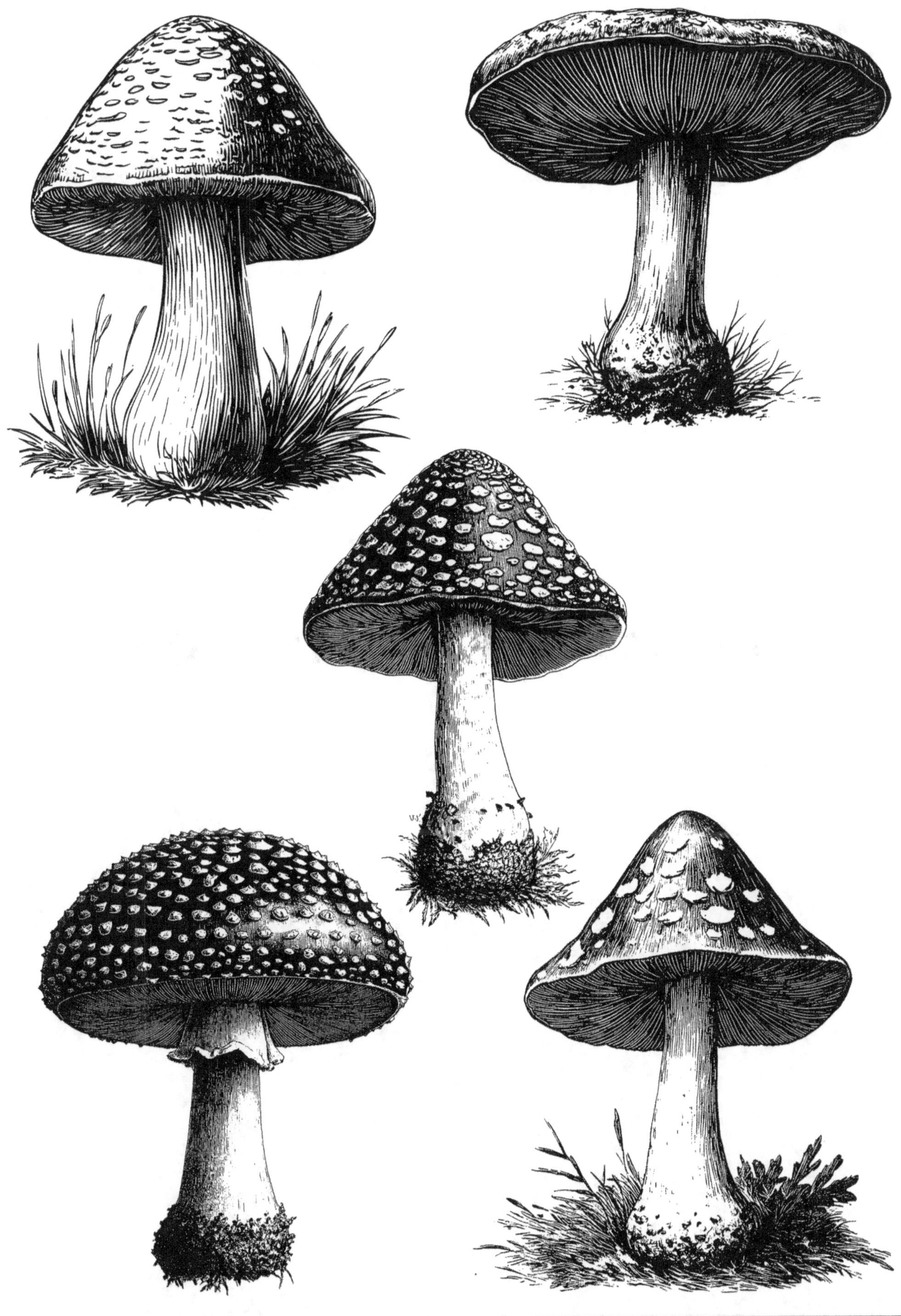

ANATOMICAL ILLUSTRATION

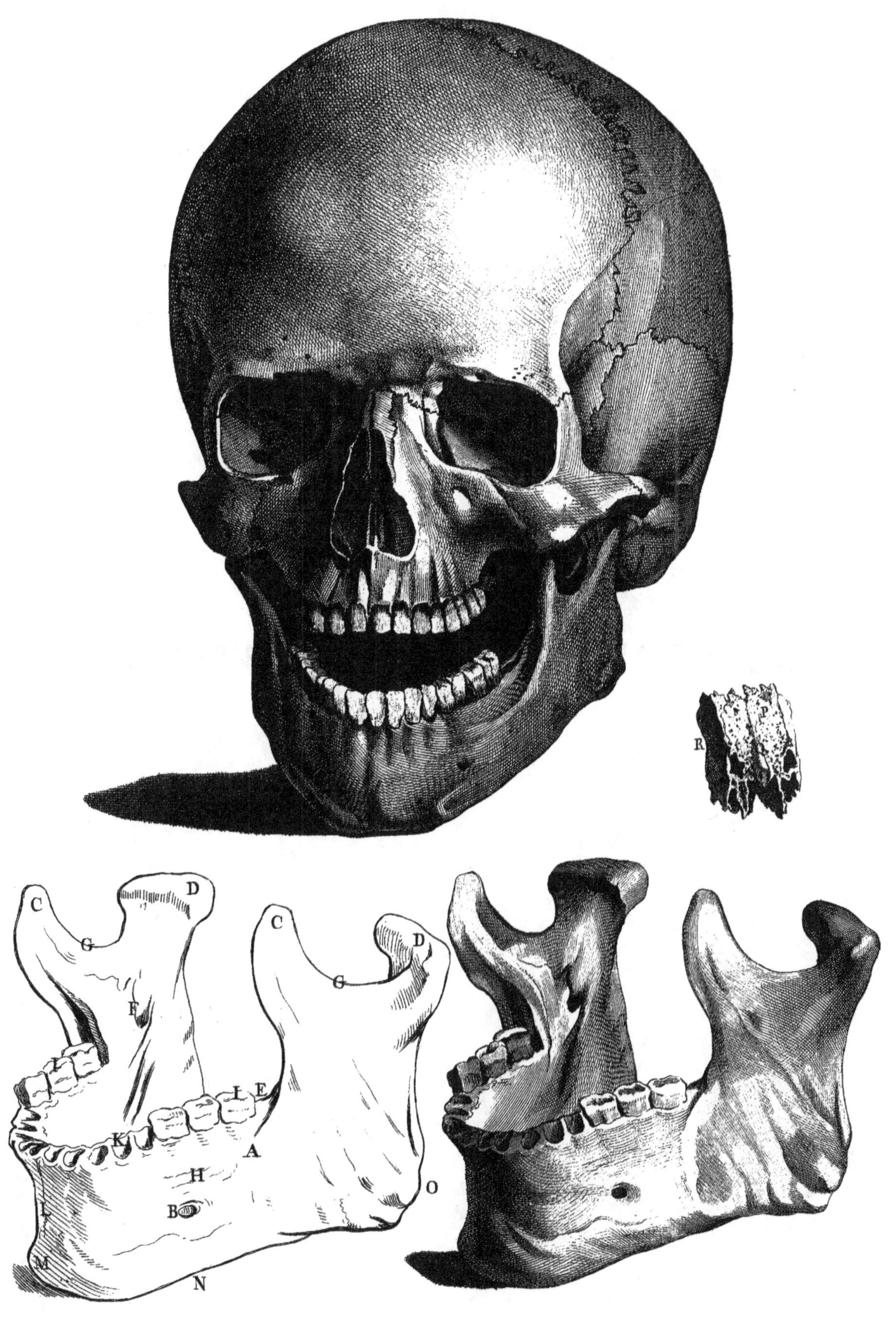

R   P
C   D
G
F
C   D
G
I E
K
A
H
L
B
M
O
N

ANATOMICAL ILLUSTRATION

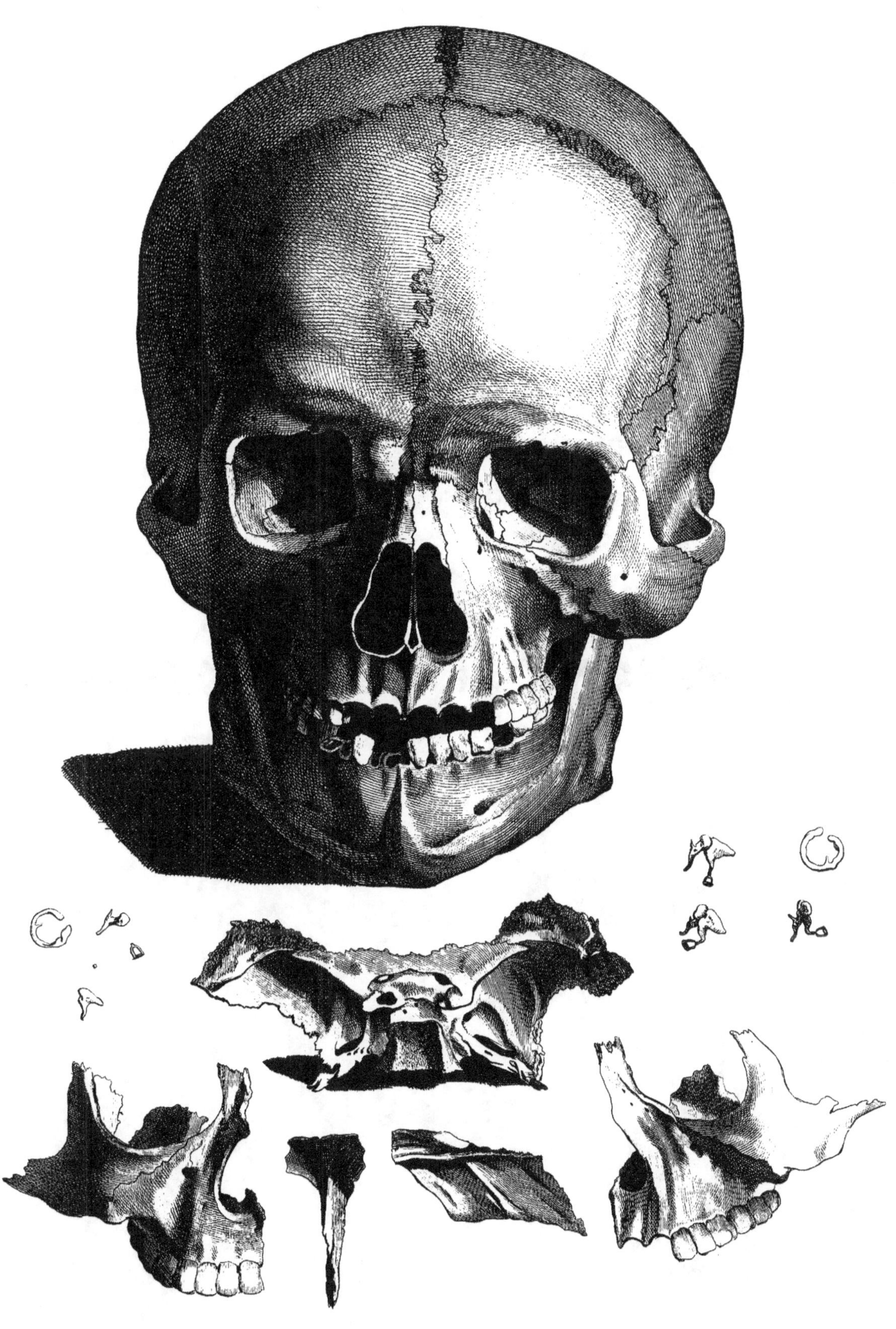

ANATOMICAL ILLUSTRATION

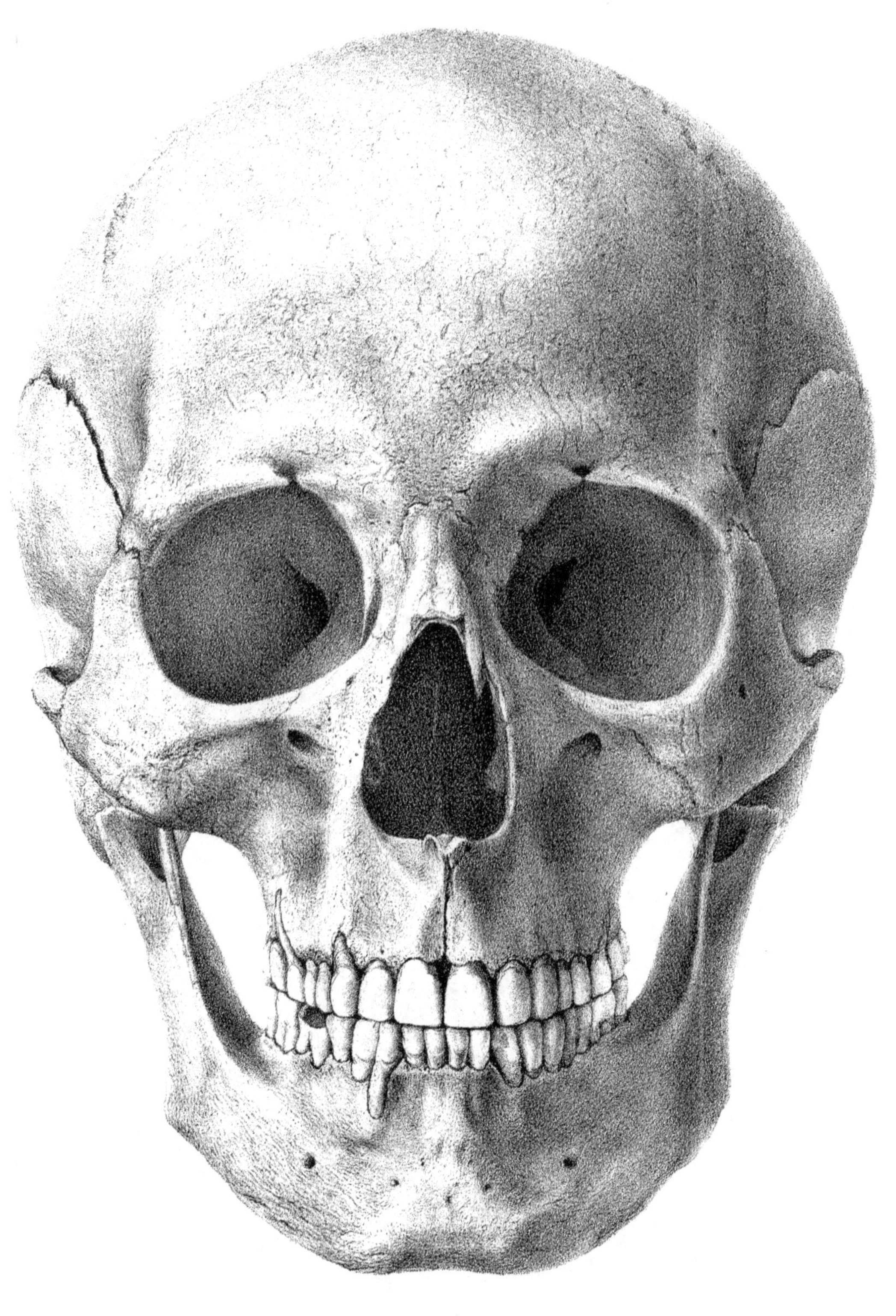

ANATOMICAL ILLUSTRATION

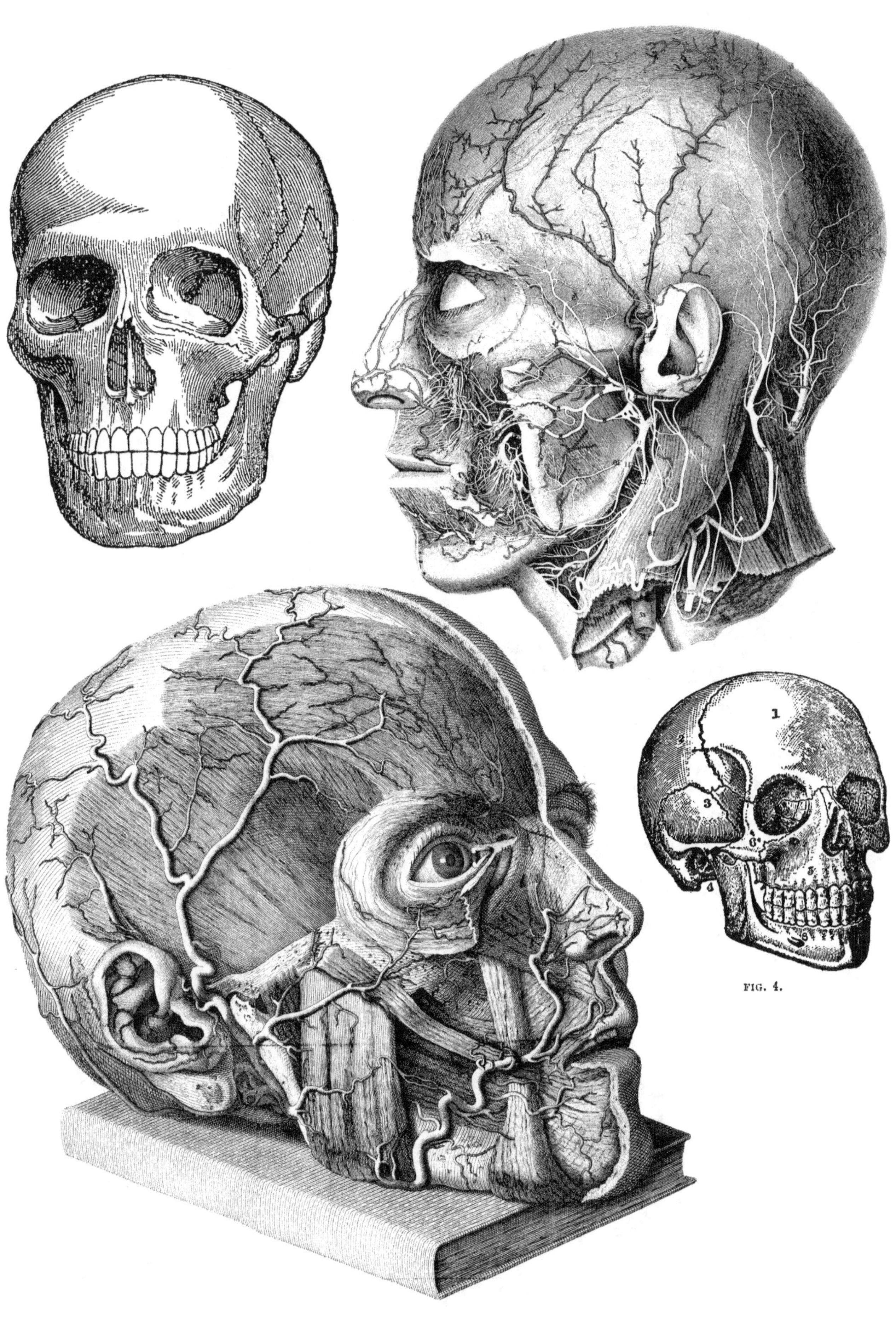

FIG. 4.

CUT & COLLAGE 3

SCULPTURE

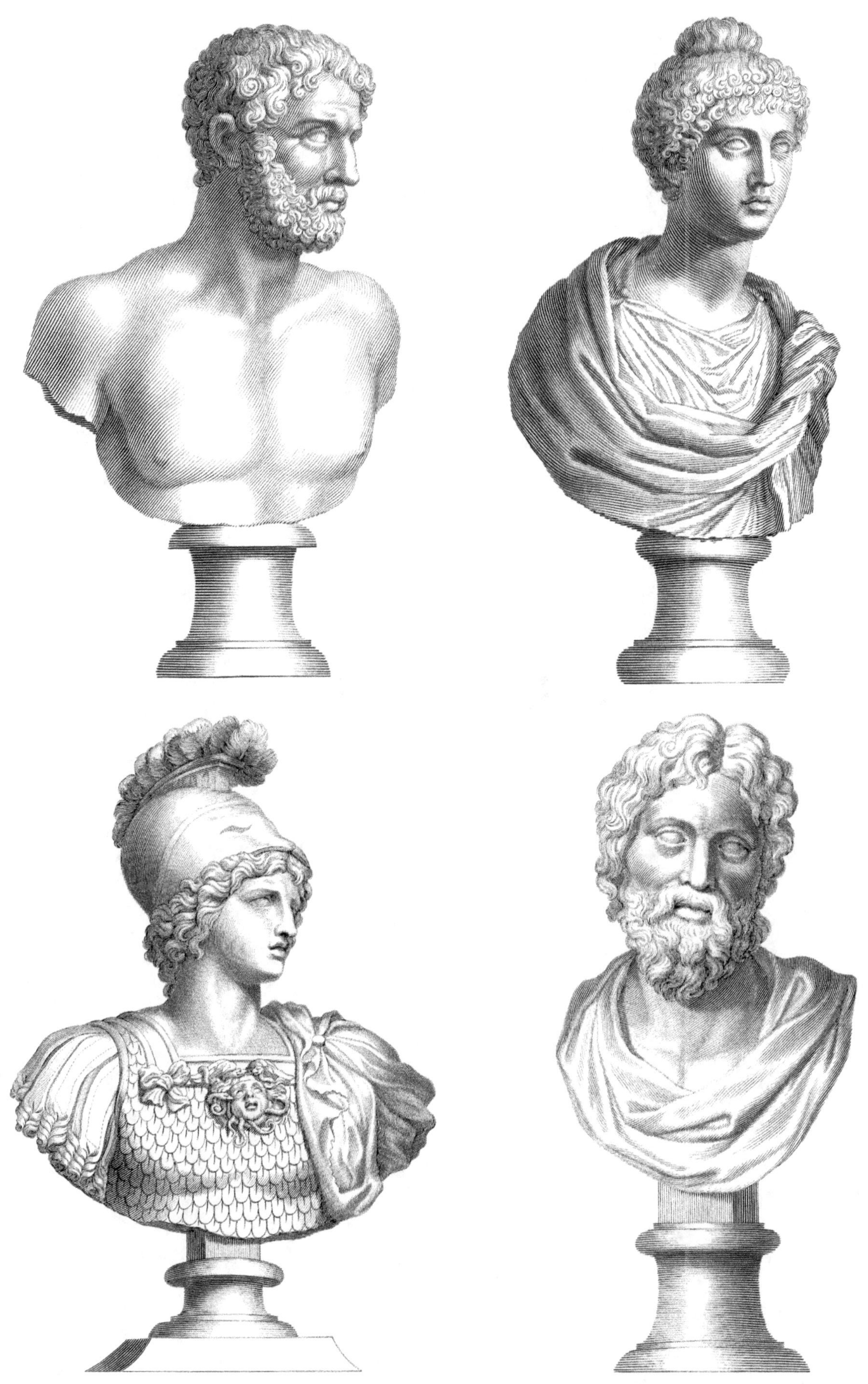

SCULPTURE

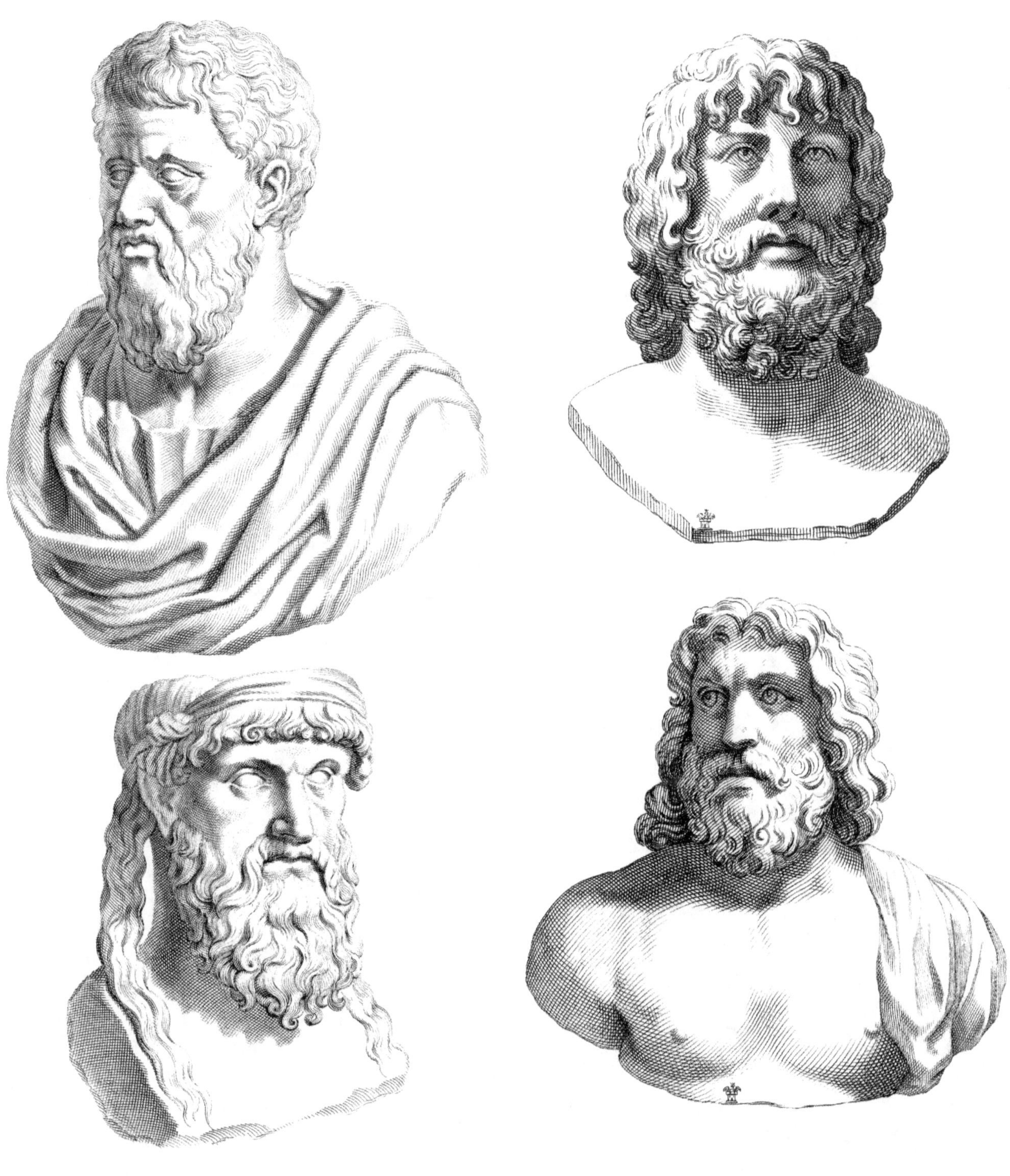

ANGELS

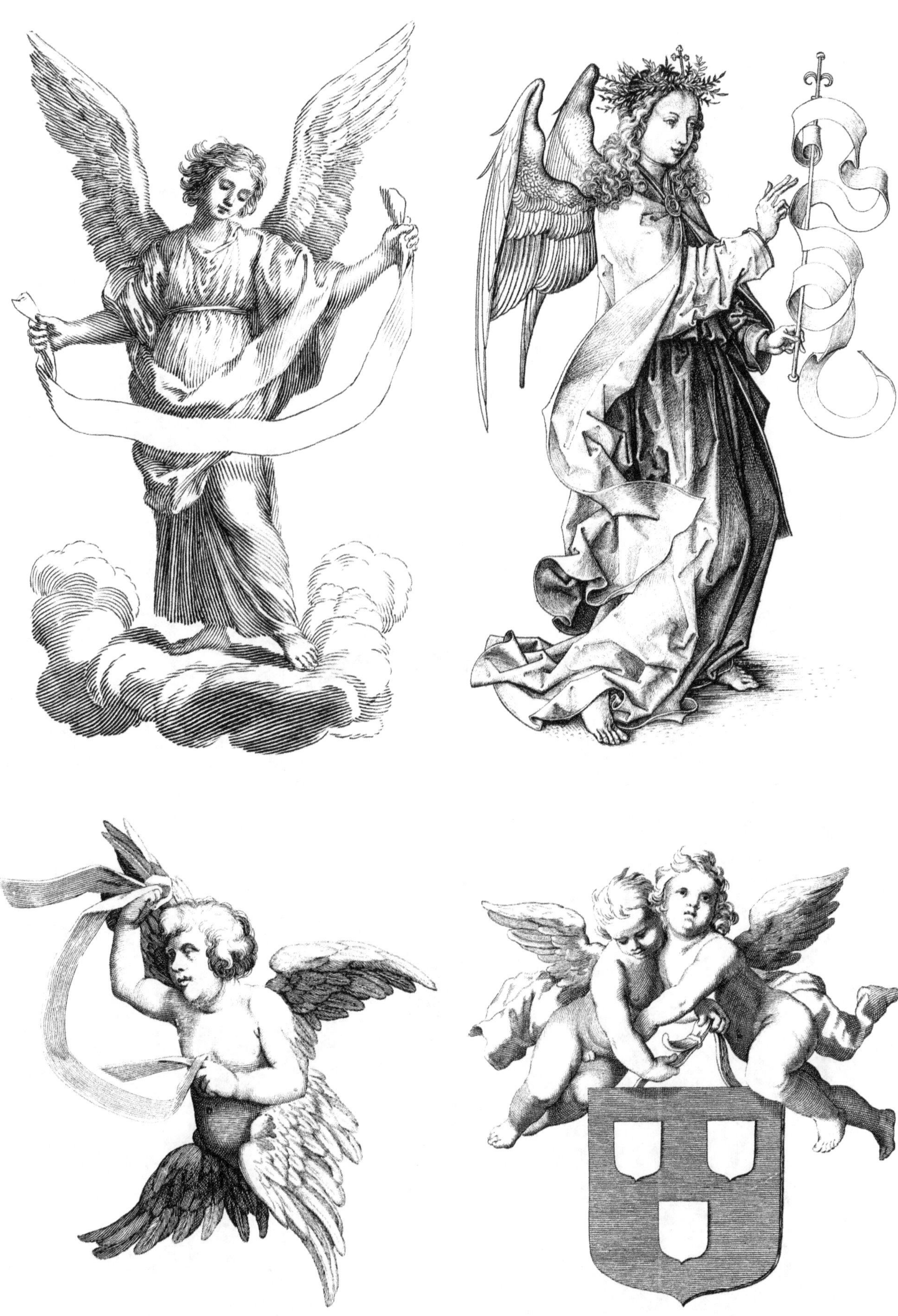

INVENTIONS

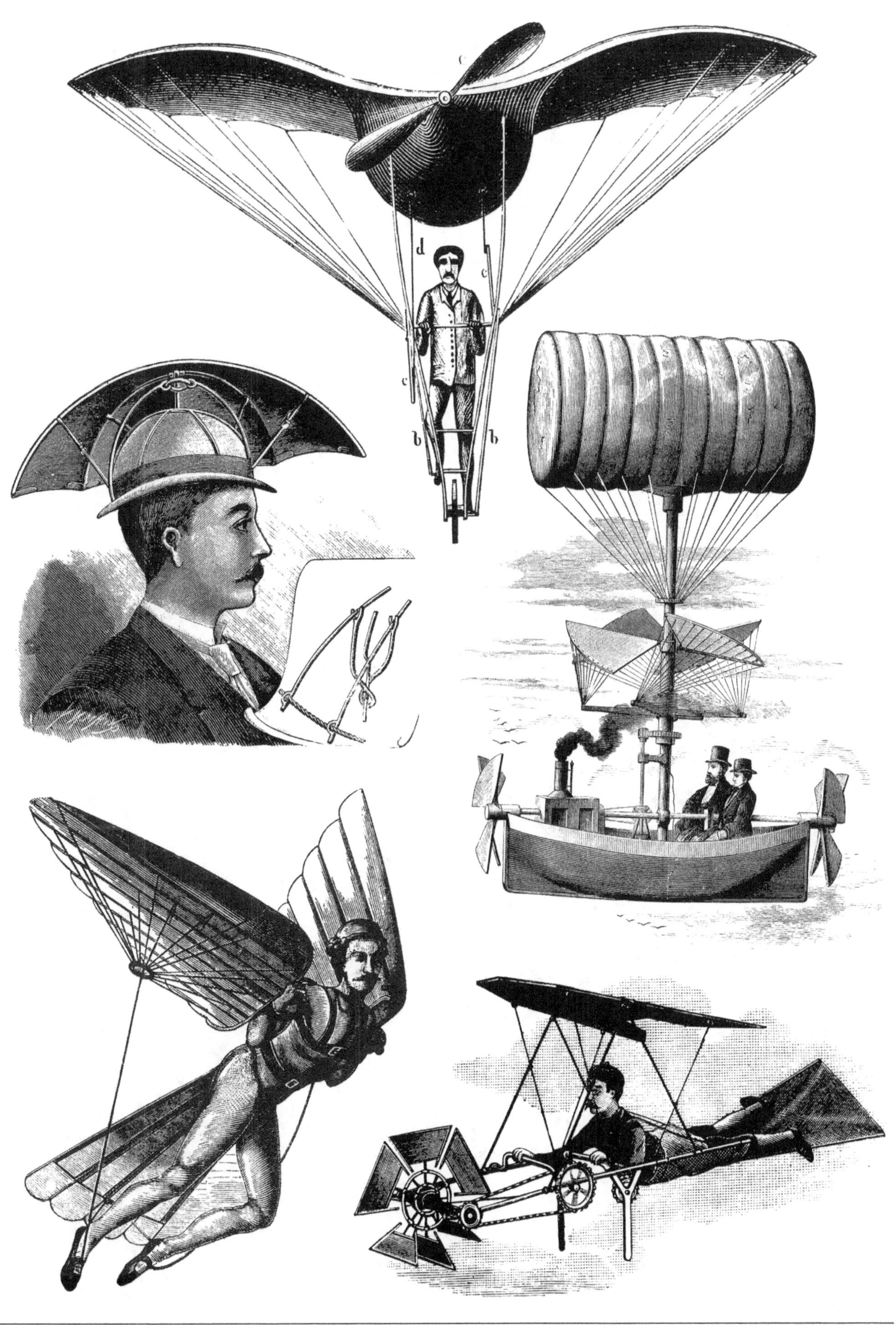

INVENTIONS

AERONAUTICS.

Plate I.

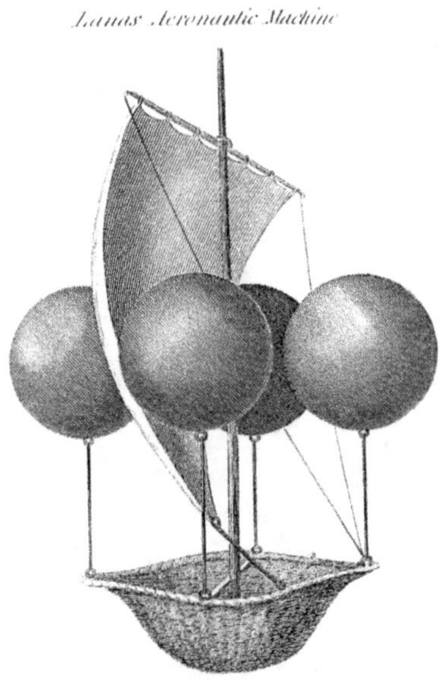
Lanas Aeronautic Machine

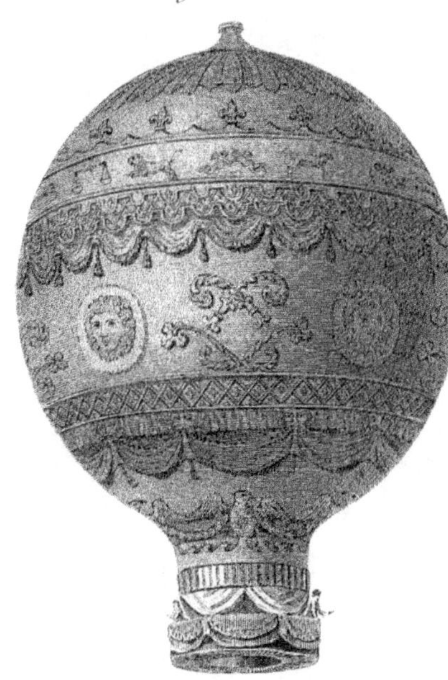
Montgolfiers Balloon

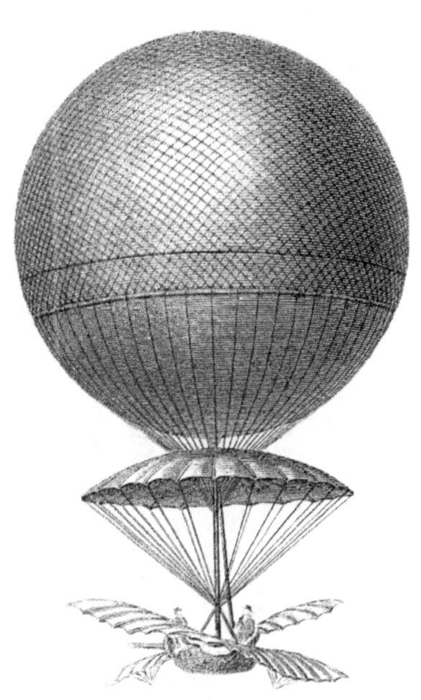
Blanchards Balloon

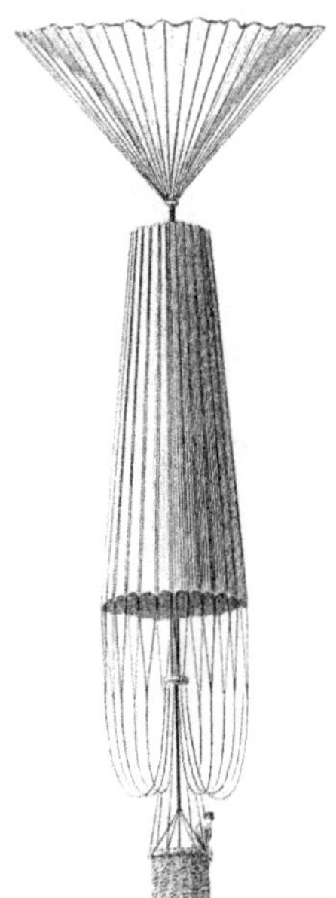
Garnerin Ascending

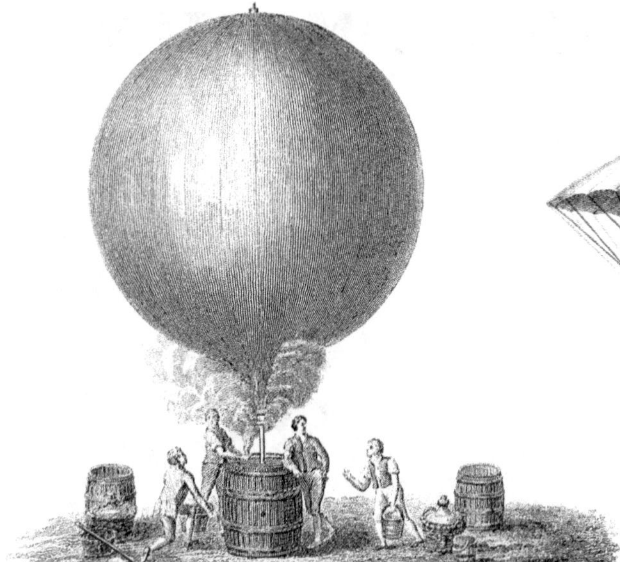
Charles & Roberts' Balloon

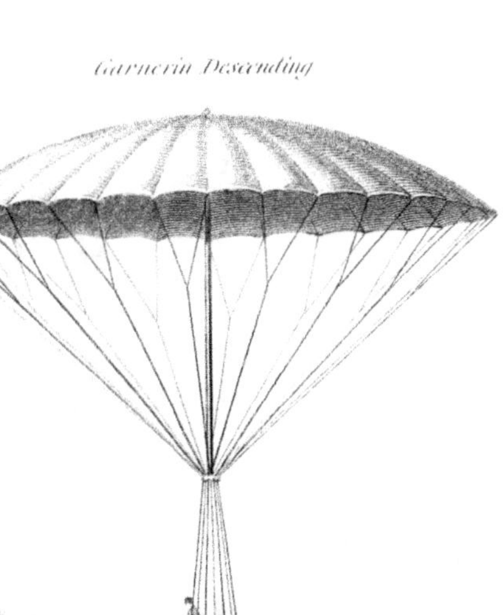
Garnerin Descending

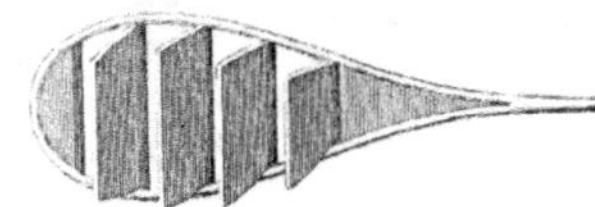
Form of the Wings employed by Lanardi

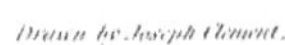

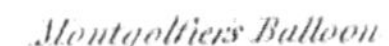
Fig. 7

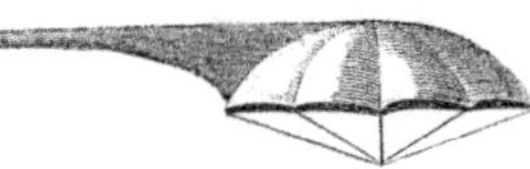
Form of the Wings employed by Blanchard

CUT & COLLAGE 3

NAUTICAL IMAGERY

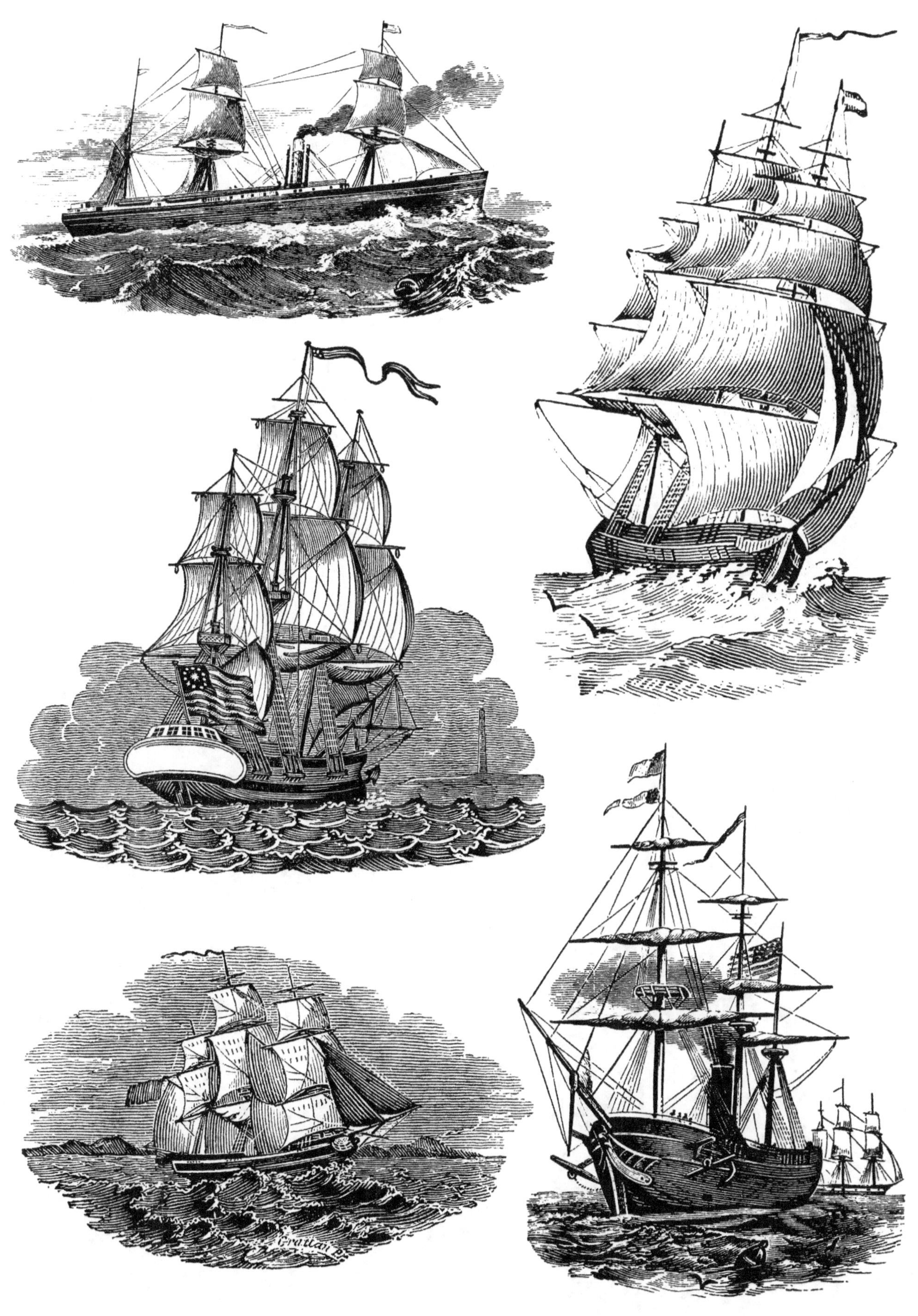

NAUTICAL IMAGERY

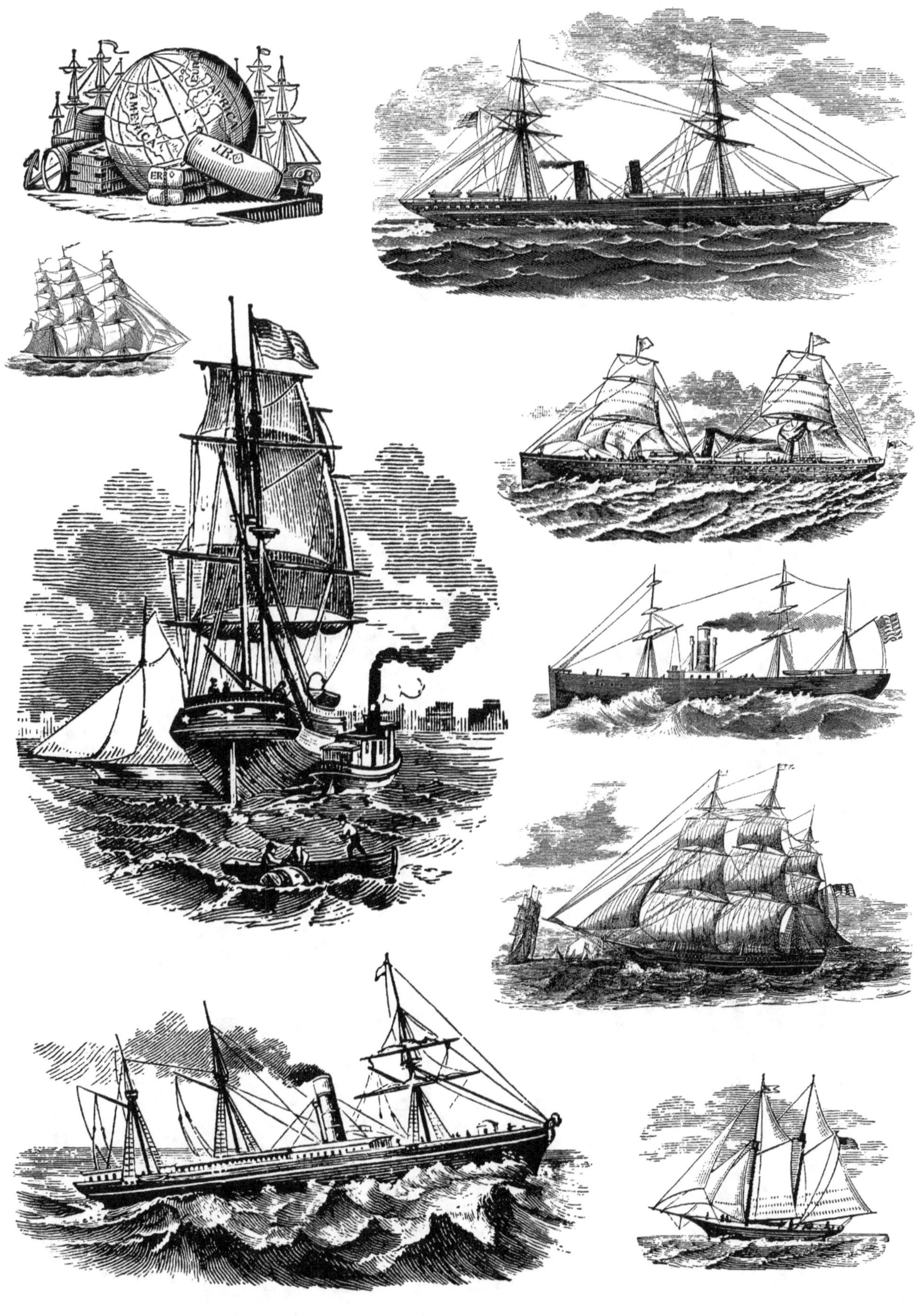

CLOCKS & WATCHES

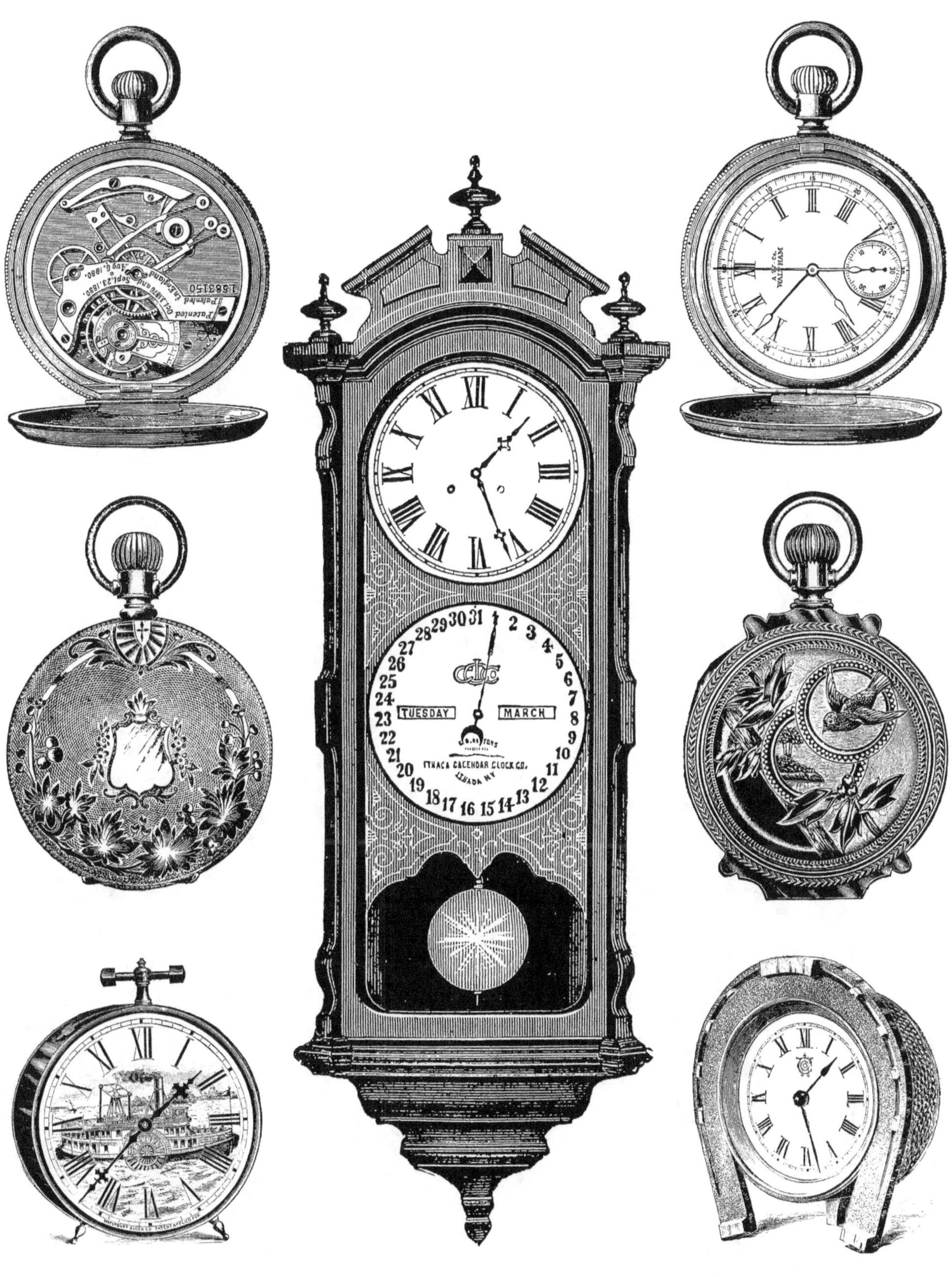

CUT & COLLAGE 3

HEARTS

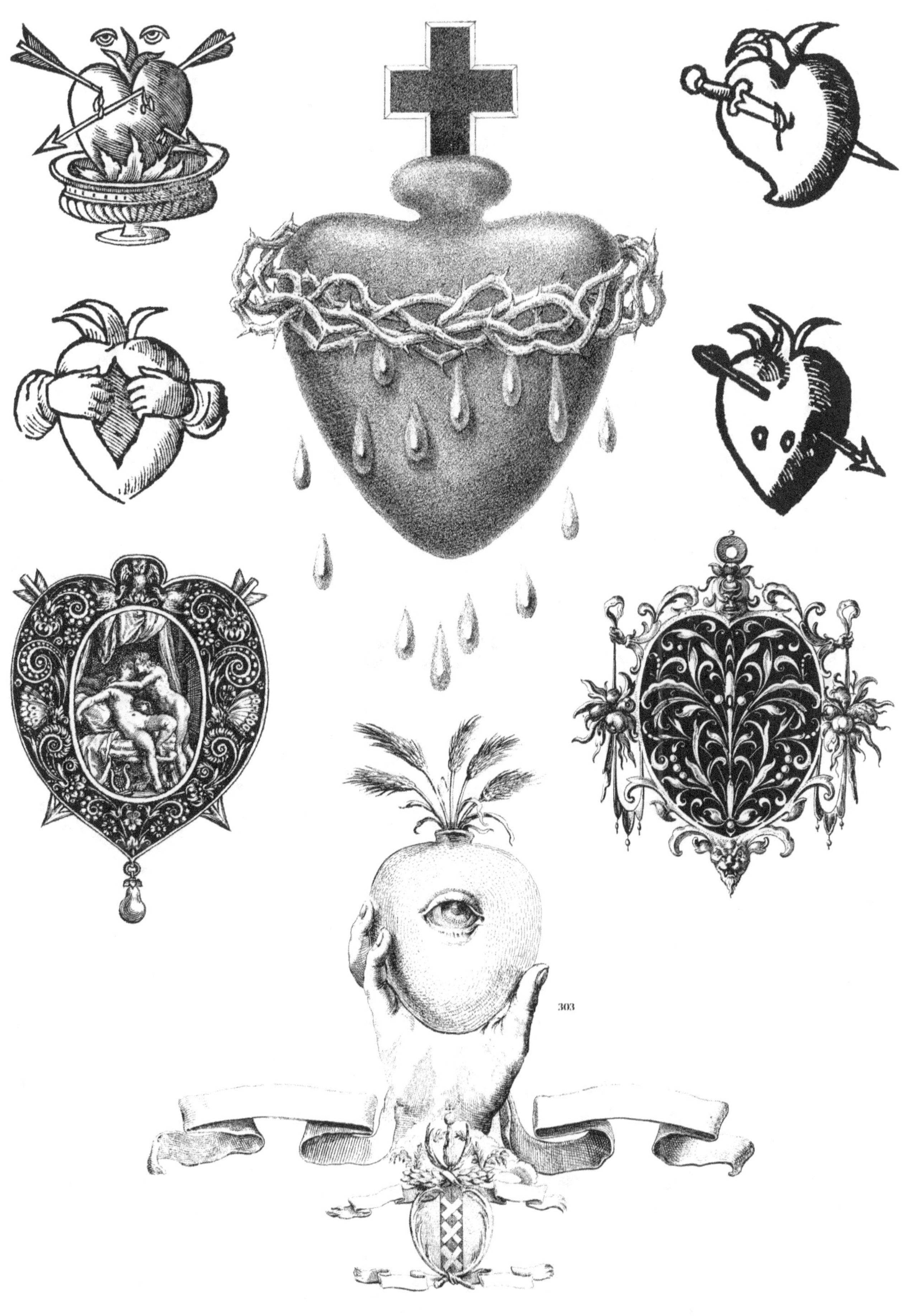

INSECTS

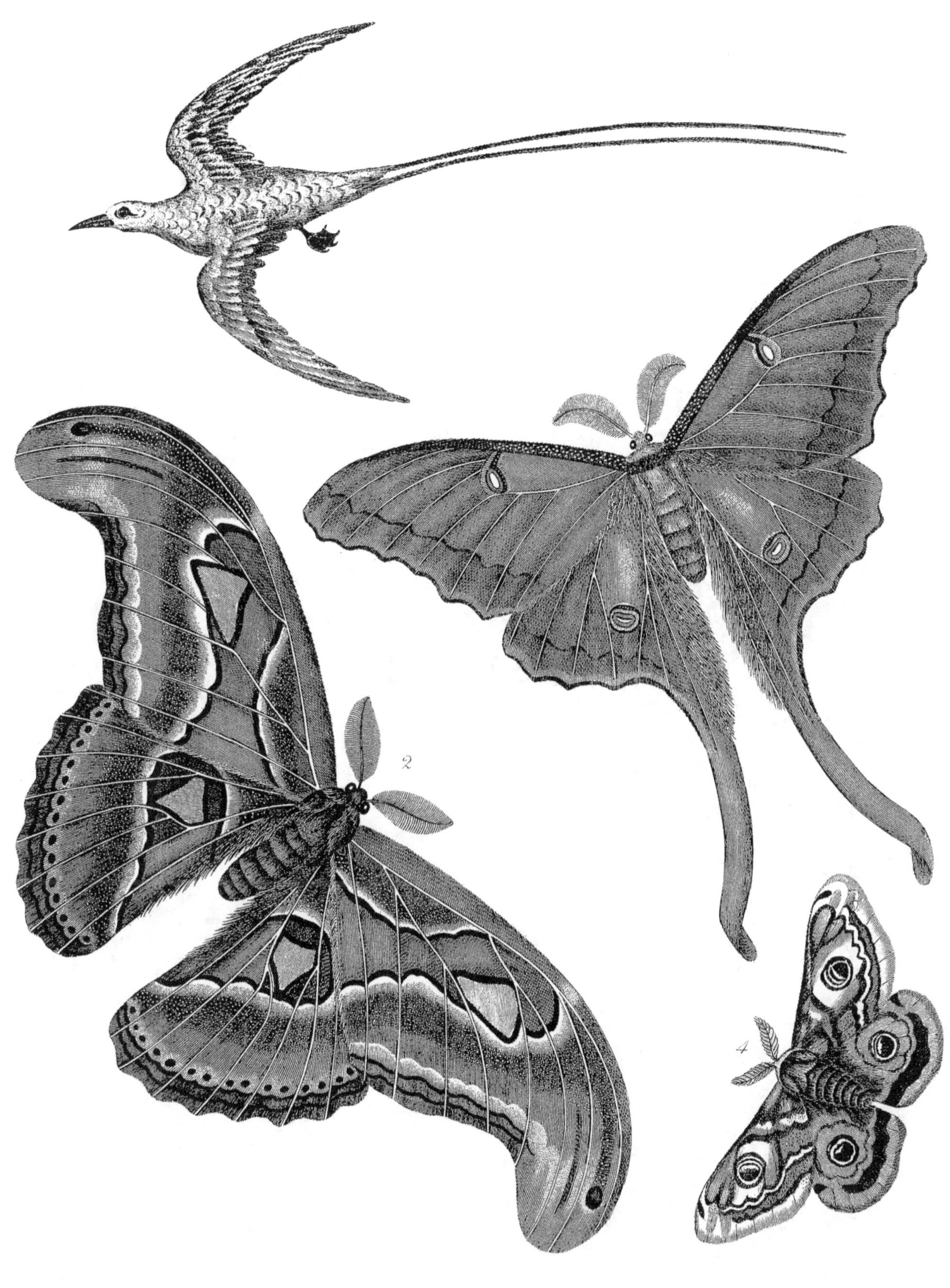

INSECTS

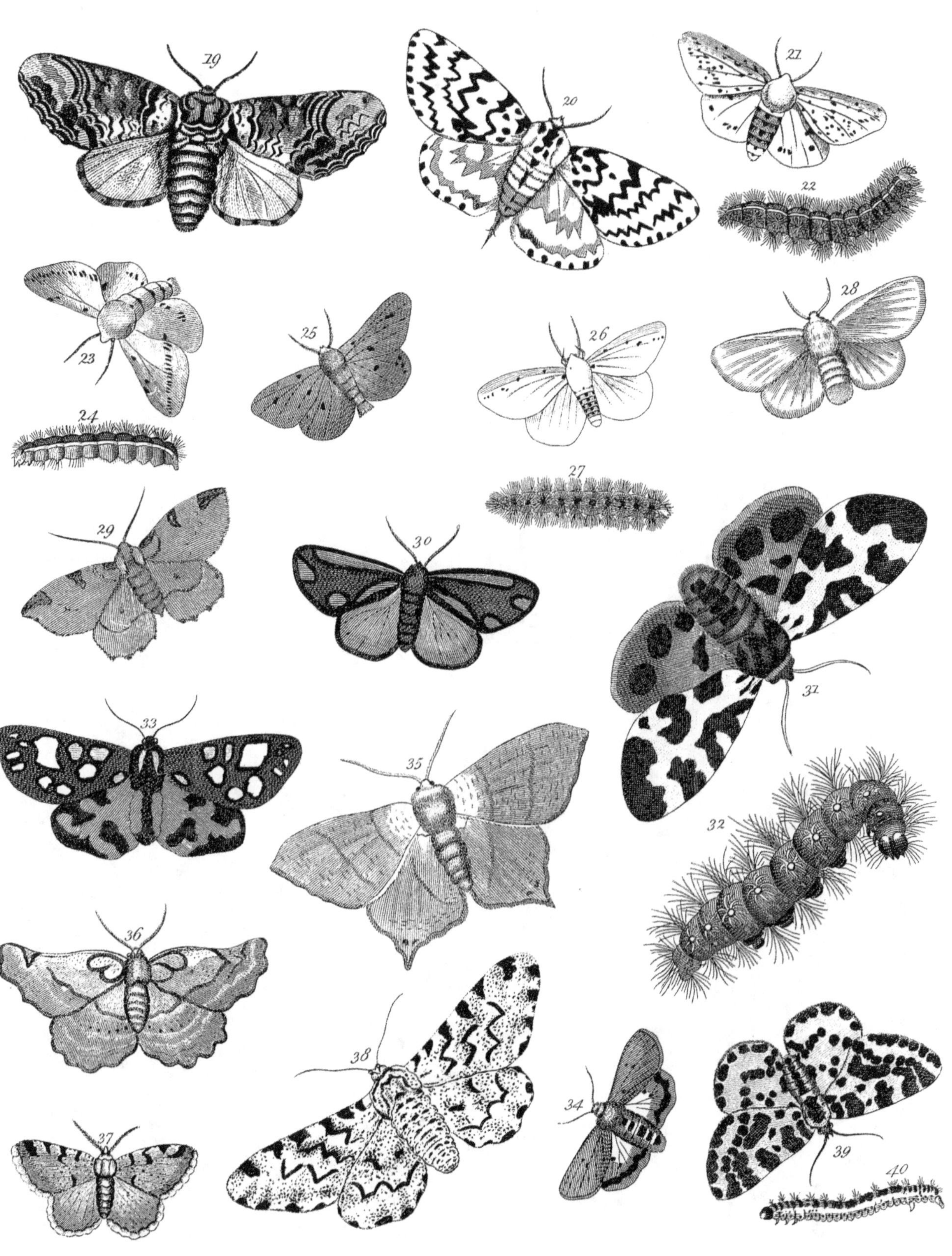

INSECTS

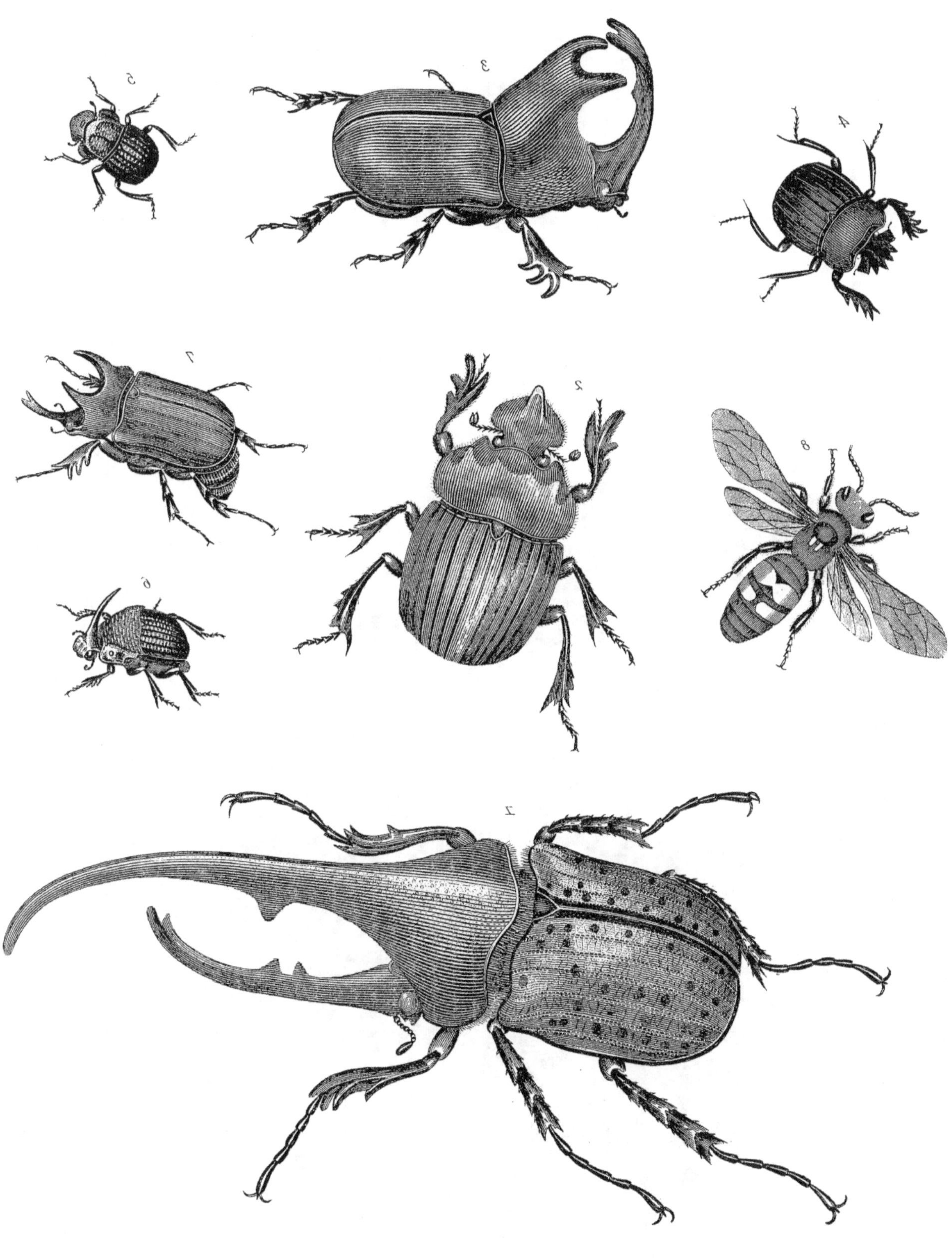

MONSTERS

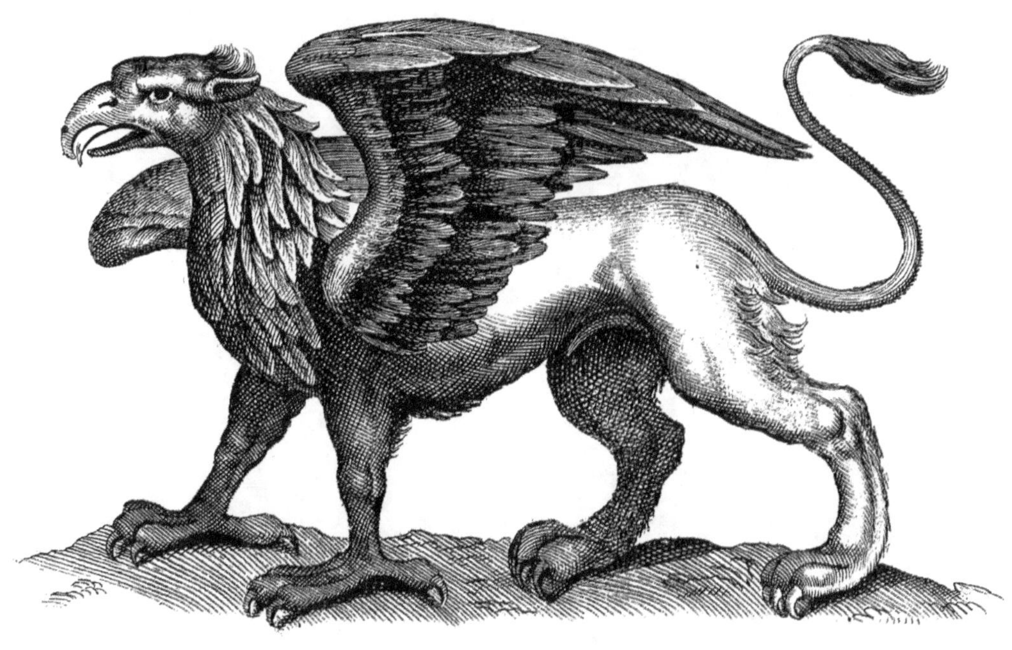

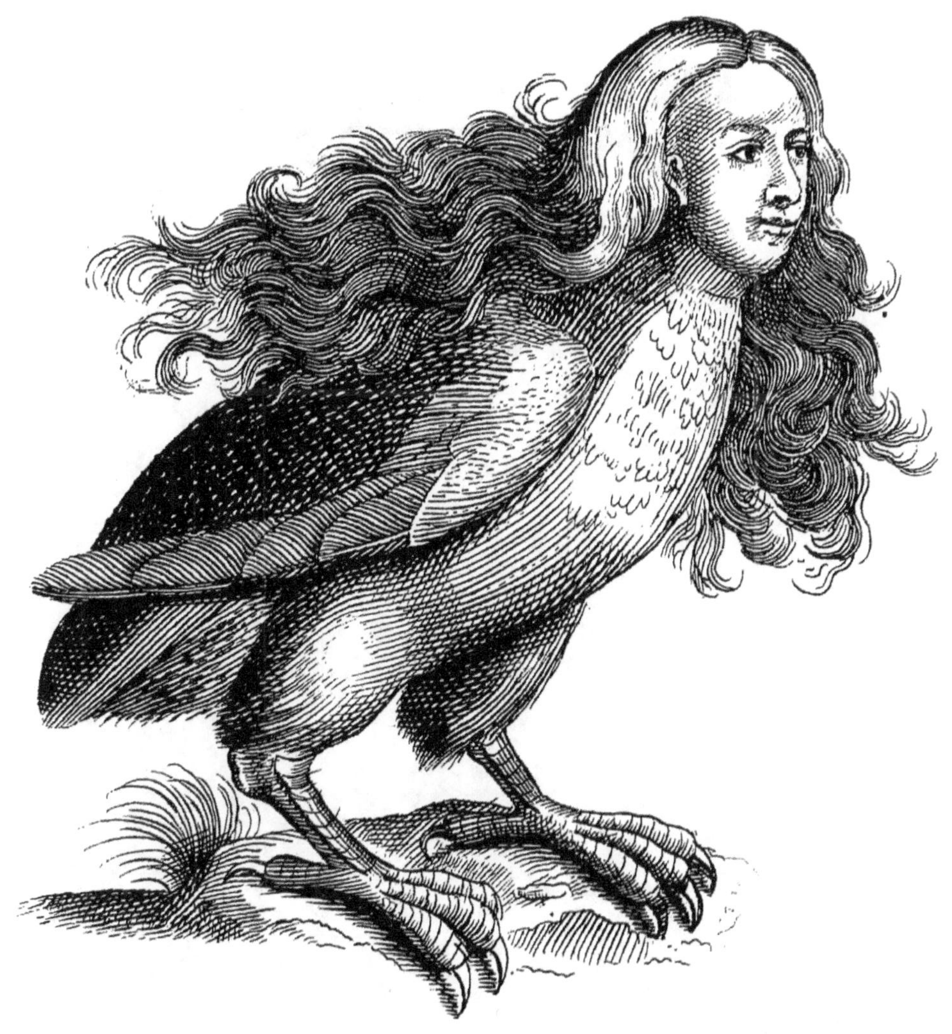

MONSTERS

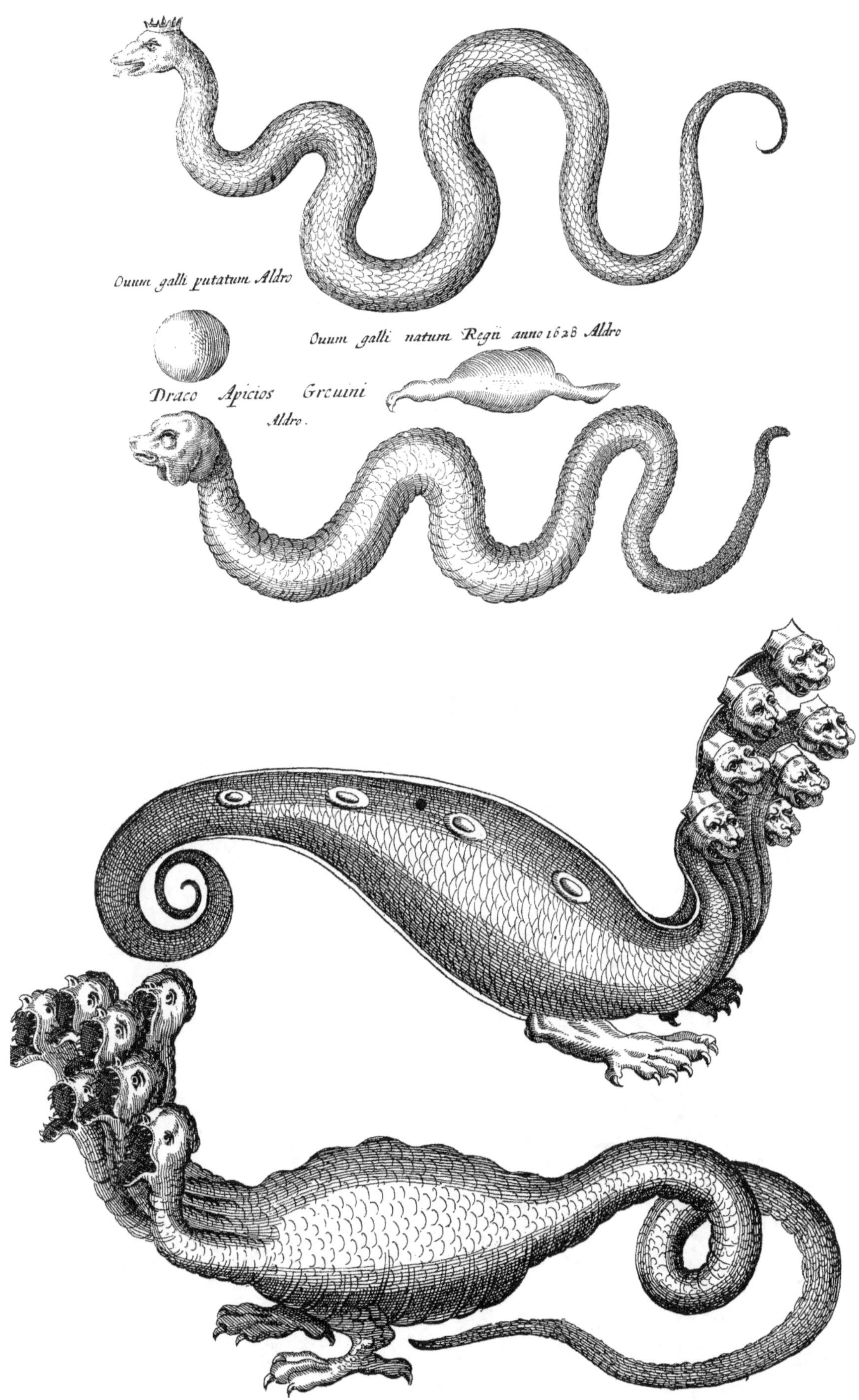
Ouum galli putatum Aldro
Ouum galli natum Regii anno 1628 Aldro
Draco Apicios Gruini
Aldro.

CUT&COLLAGE3

MONSTERS

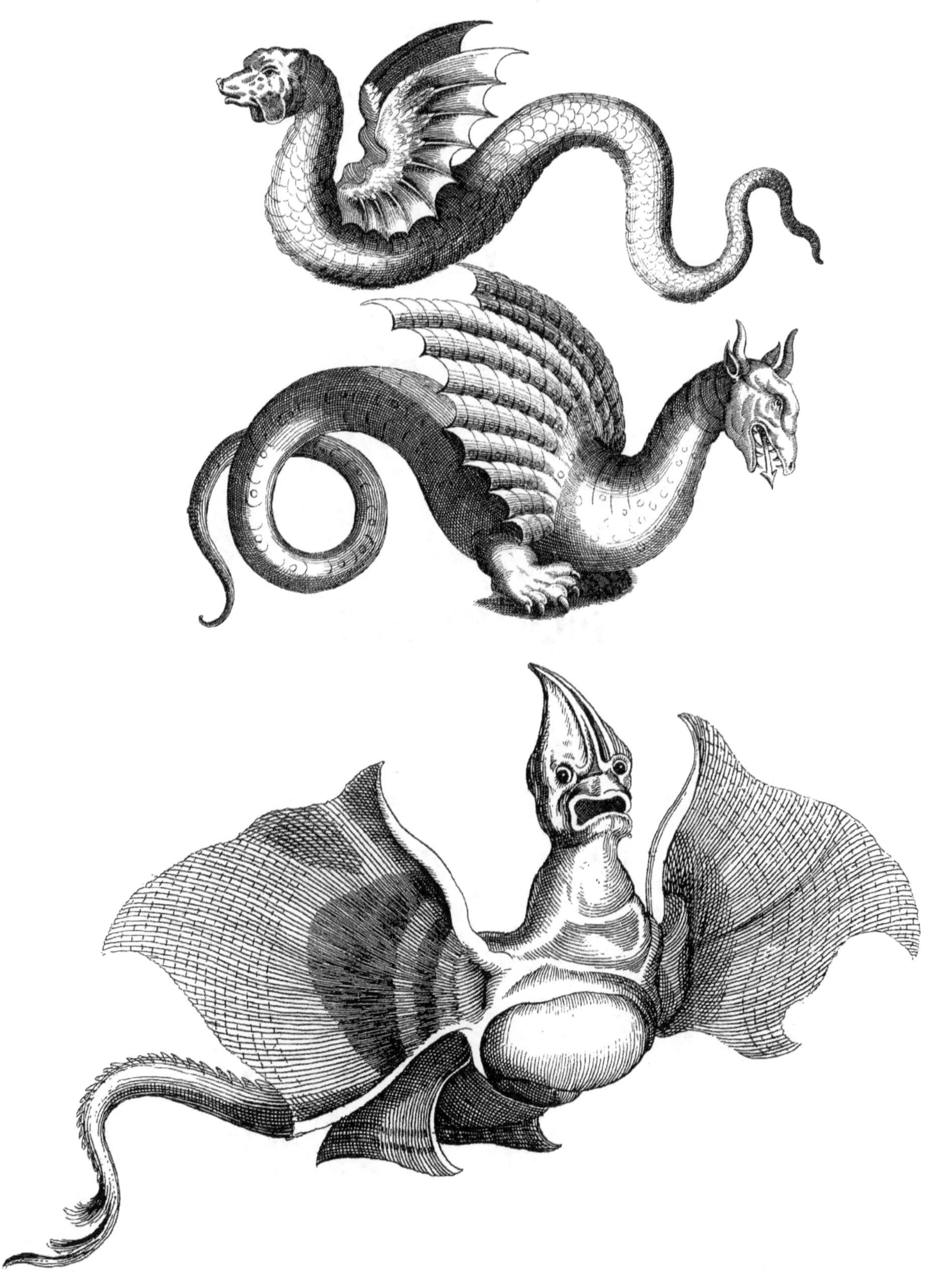

MONSTERS

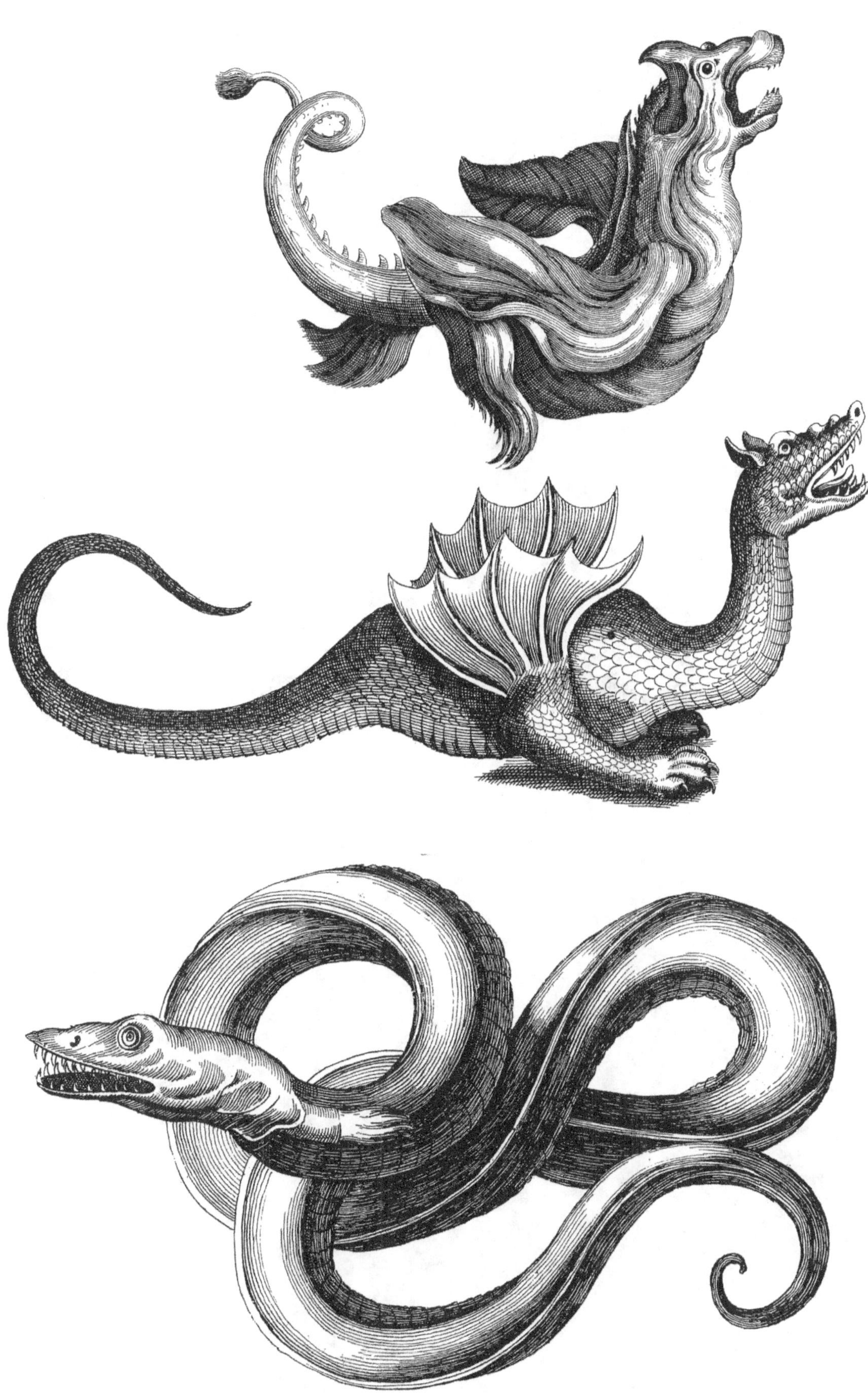

ARMS & ARMOUR

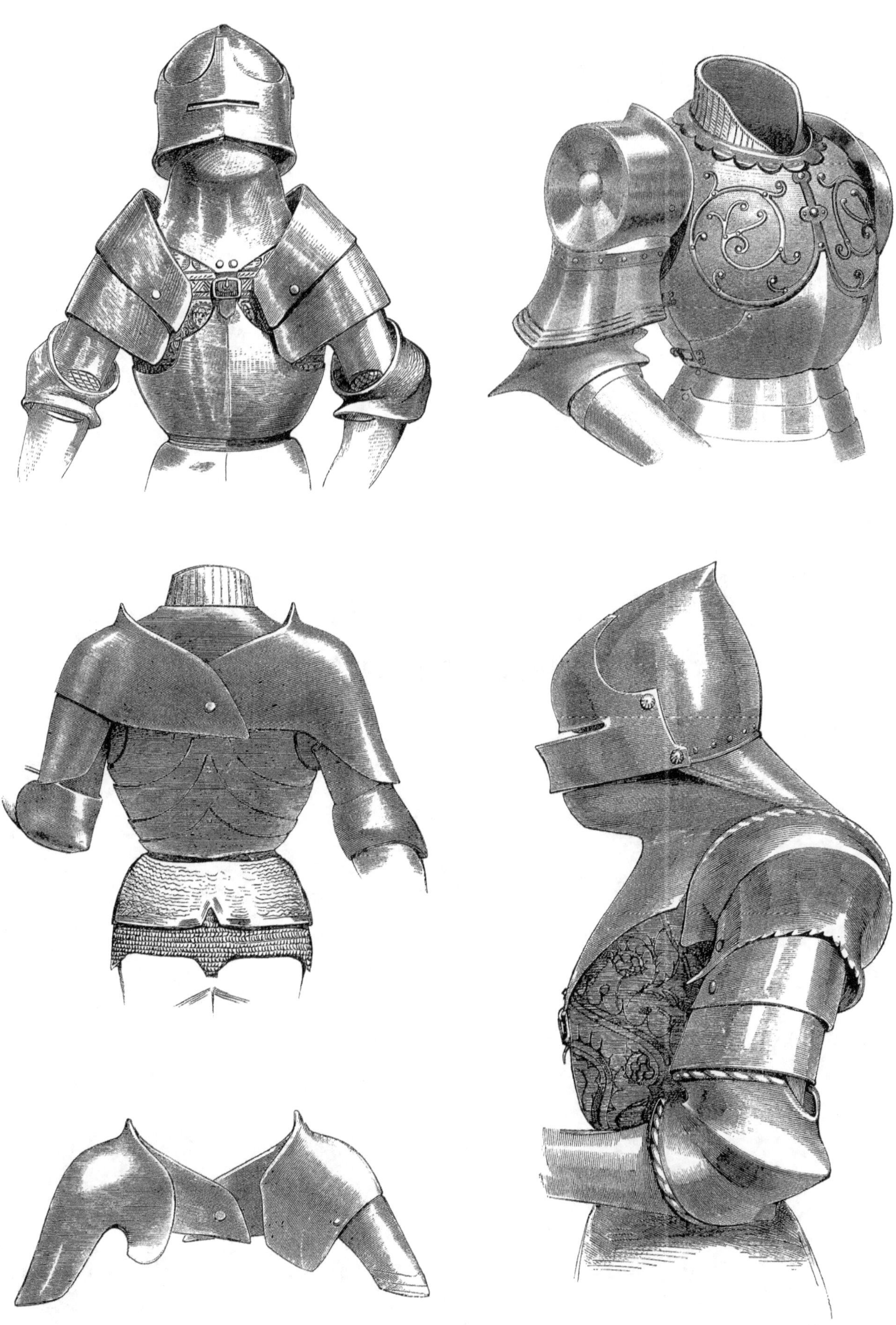

ARMS & ARMOUR

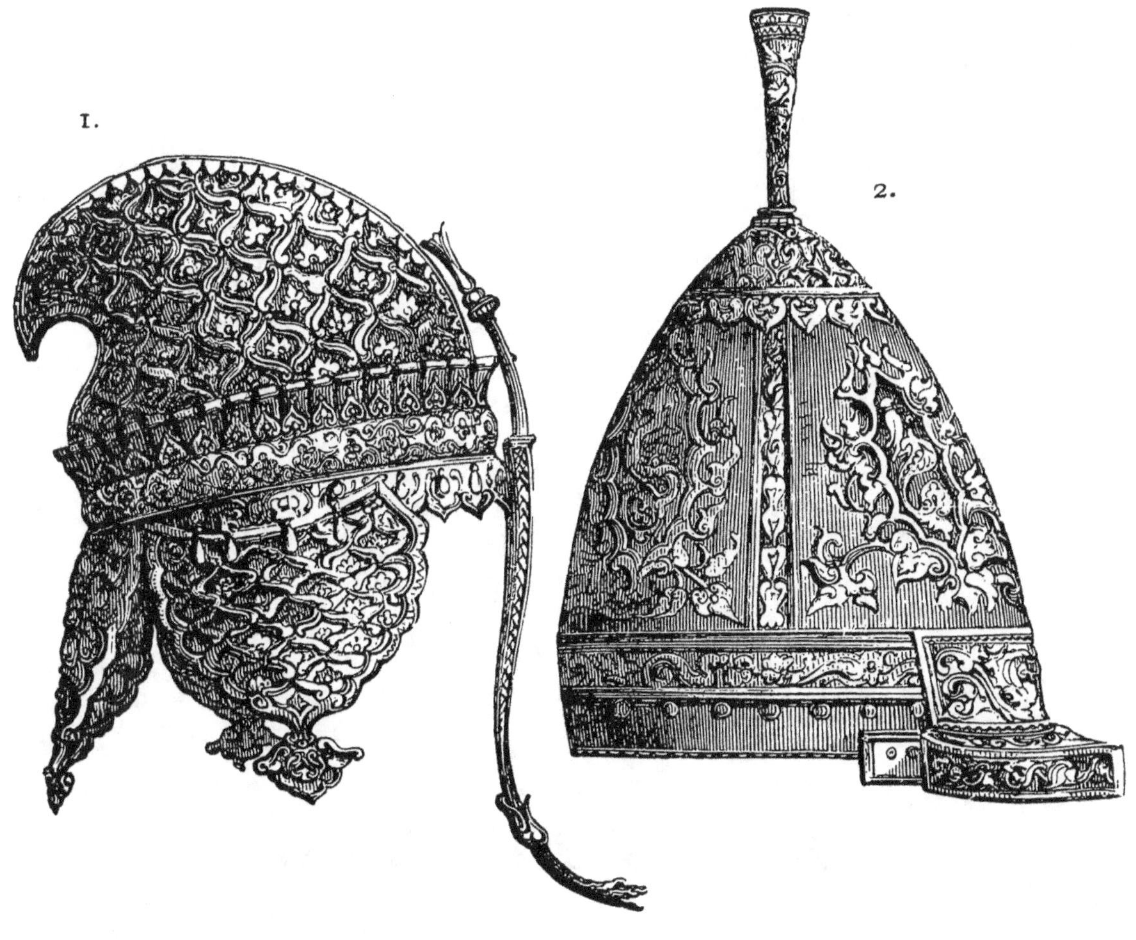

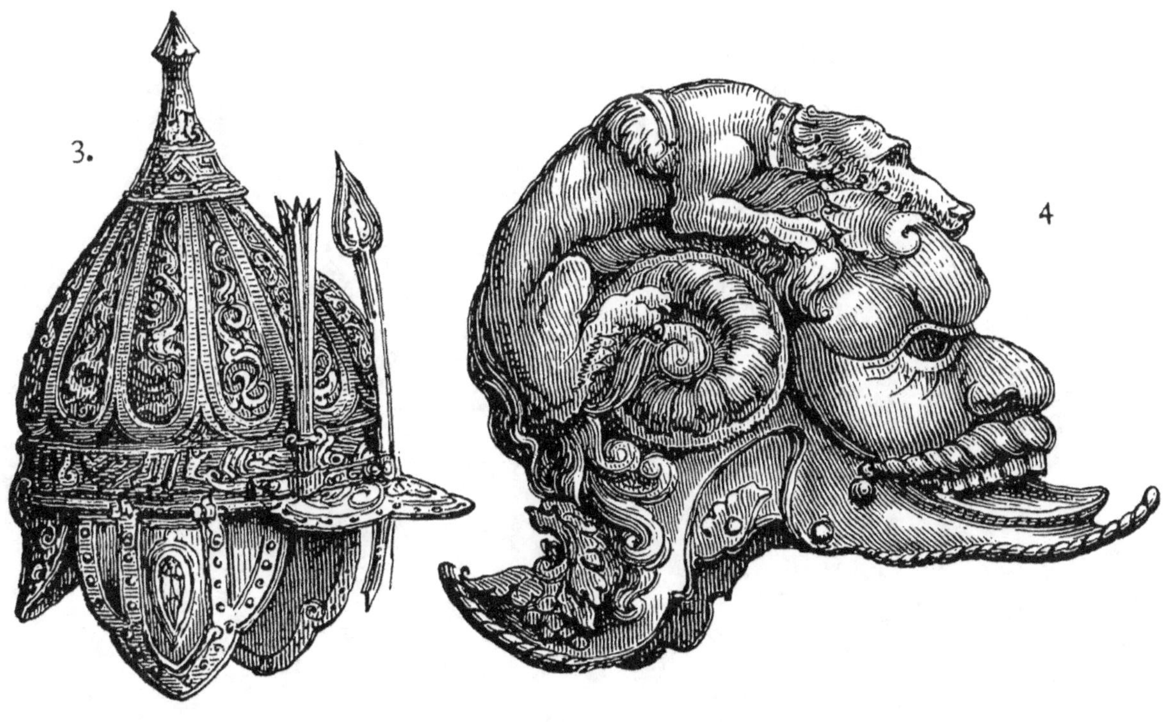

ARMS & ARMOUR

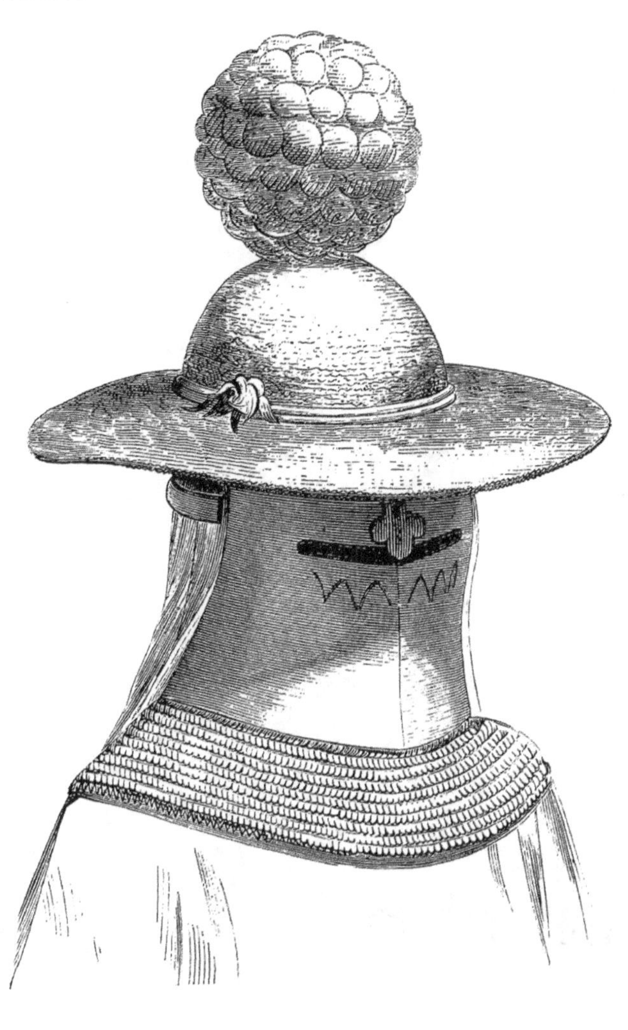

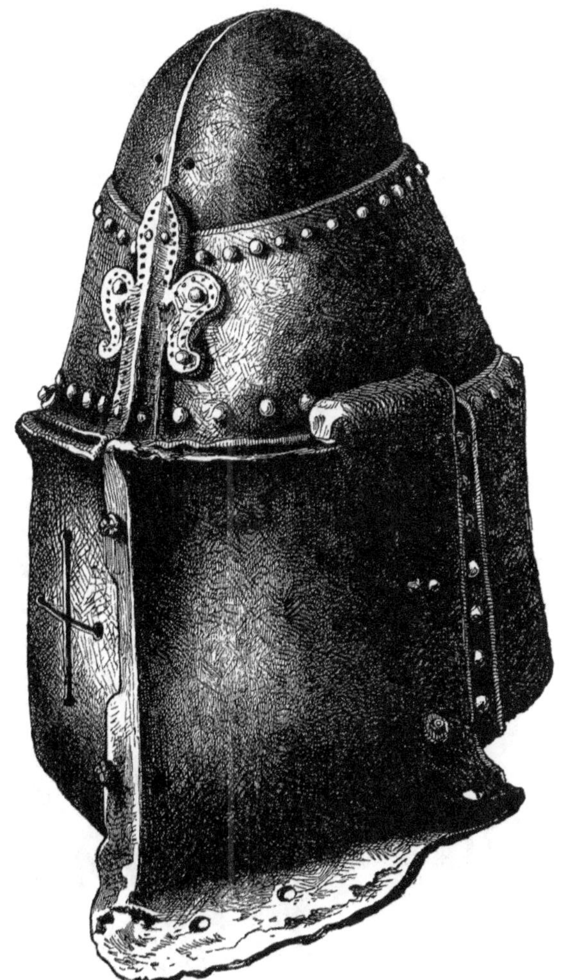

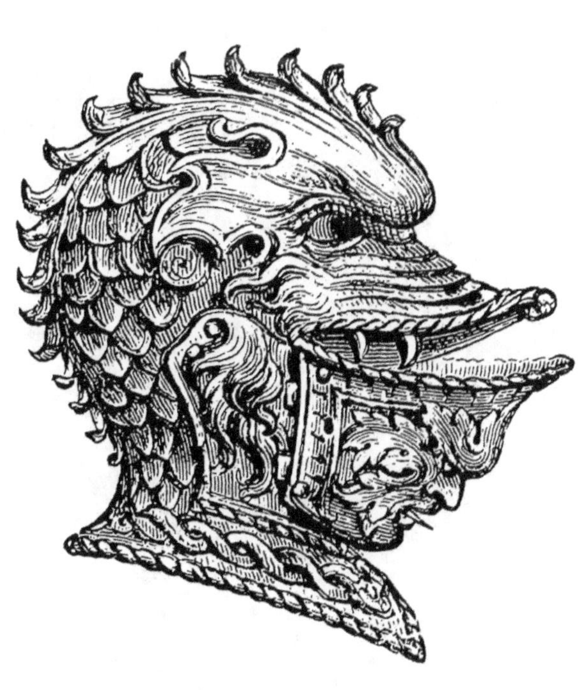

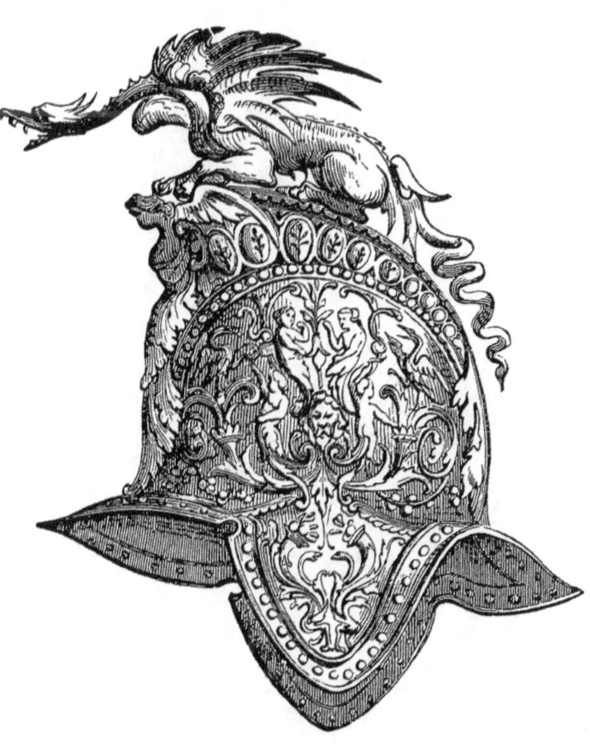

CUT & COLLAGE 3

ARMS & ARMOUR

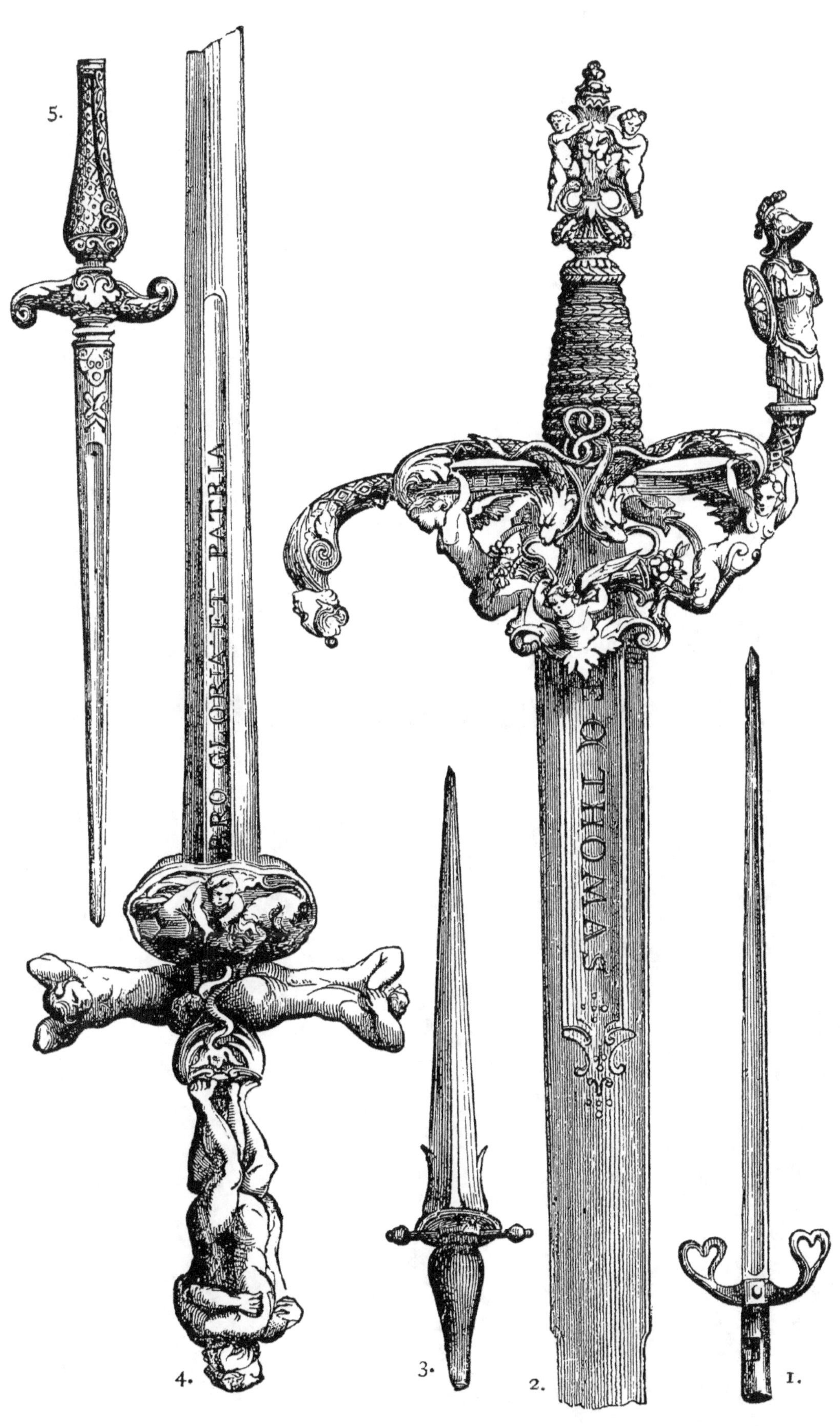

5.

4.   3.   2.   I.

ARMS & ARMOUR

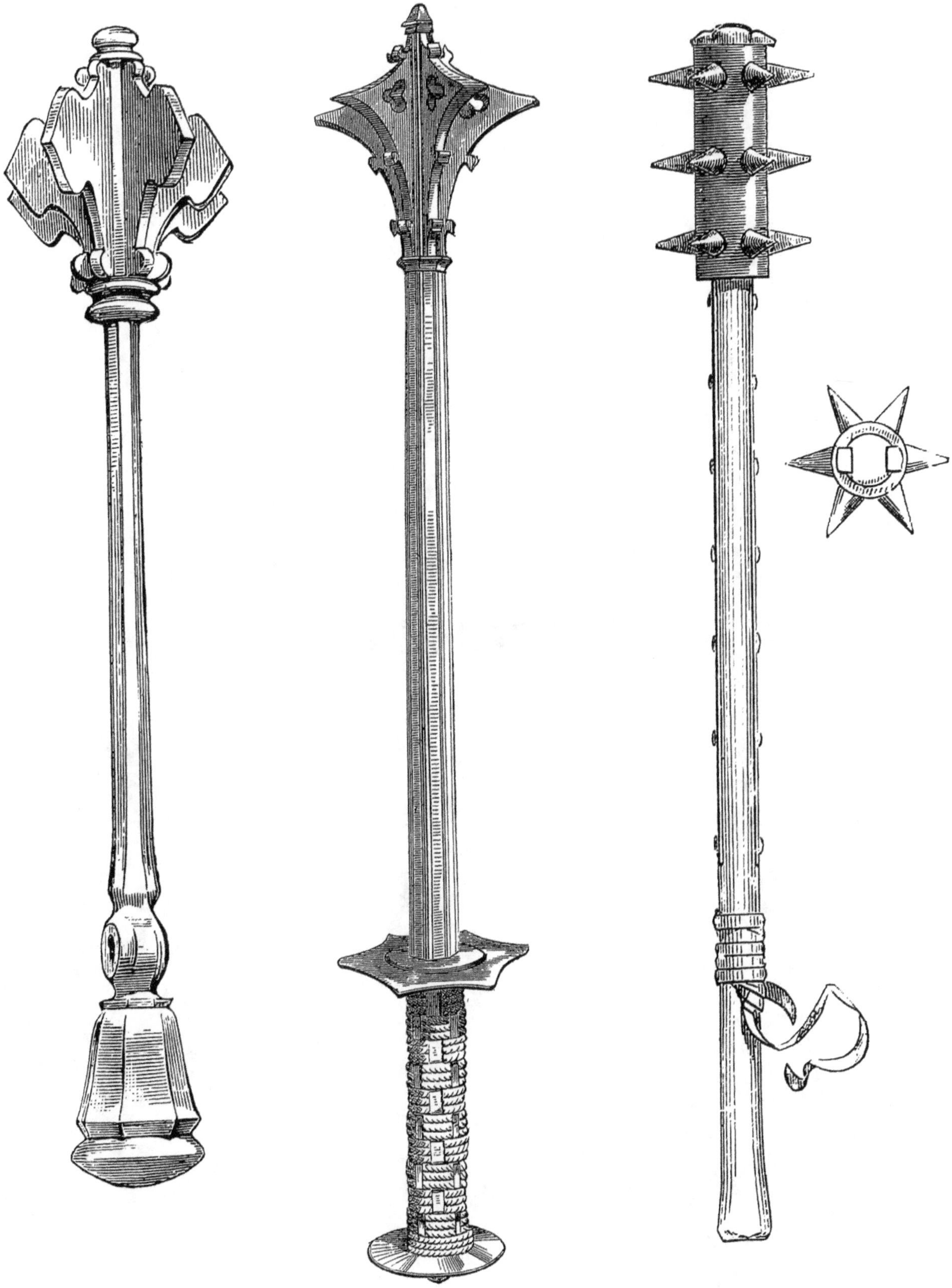

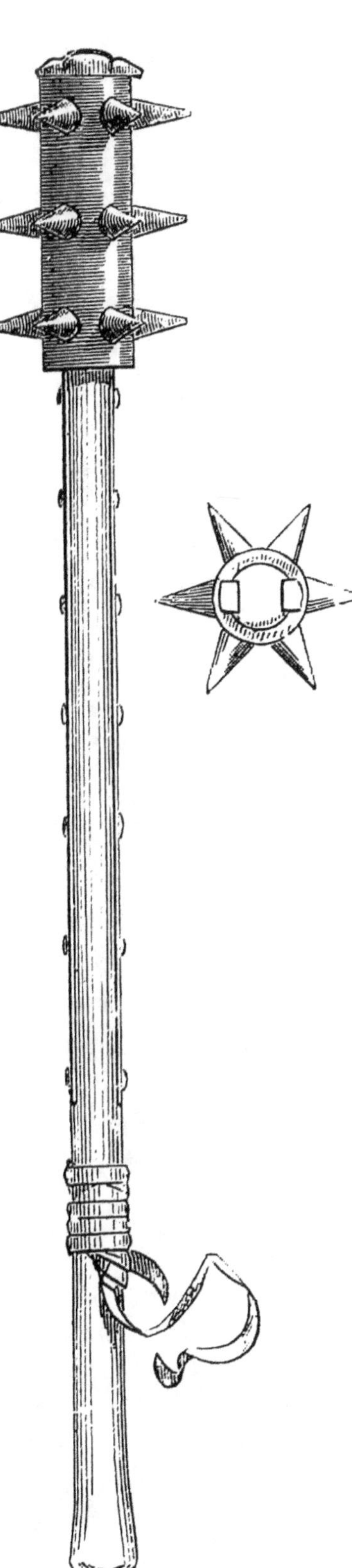

CUT & COLLAGE 3

FRAMES

FRAMES

FRAMES

ORNAMENTS

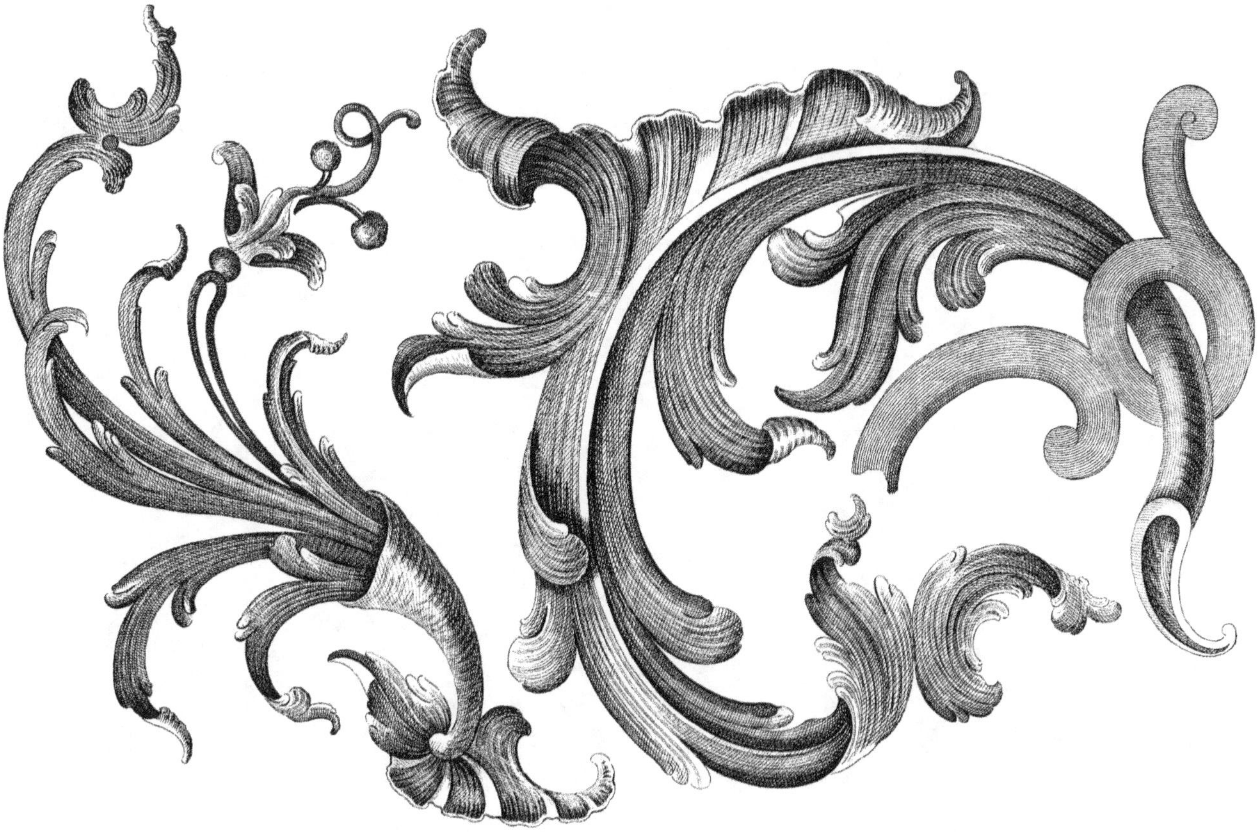

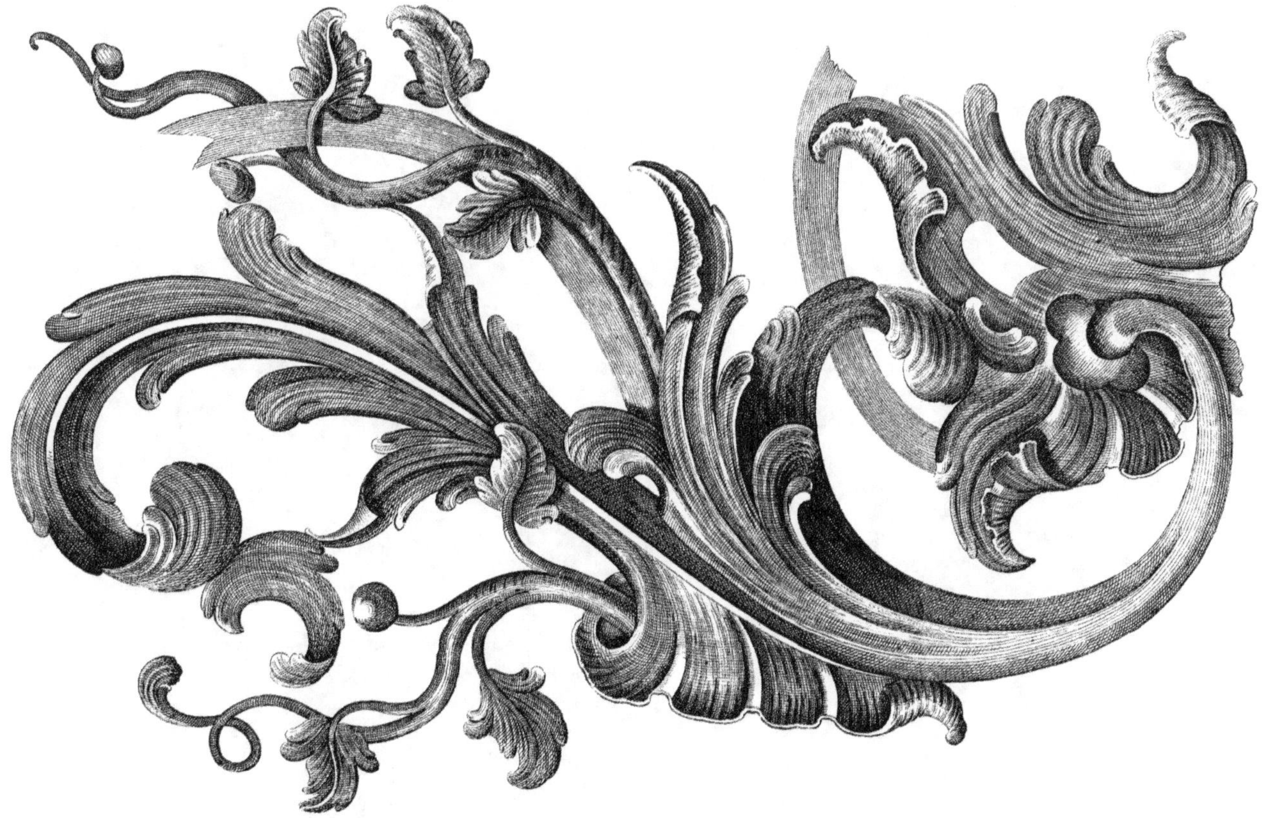

ORNAMENTS

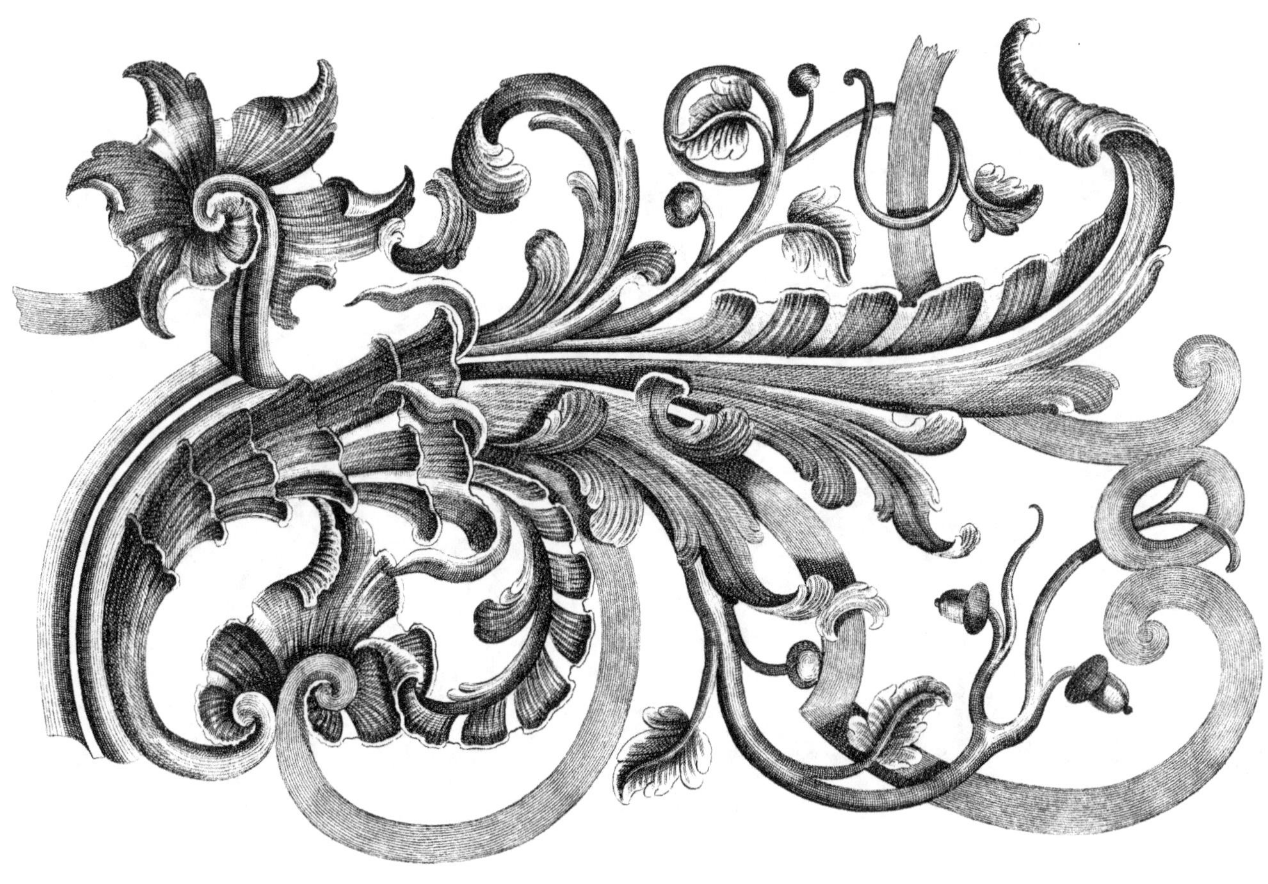

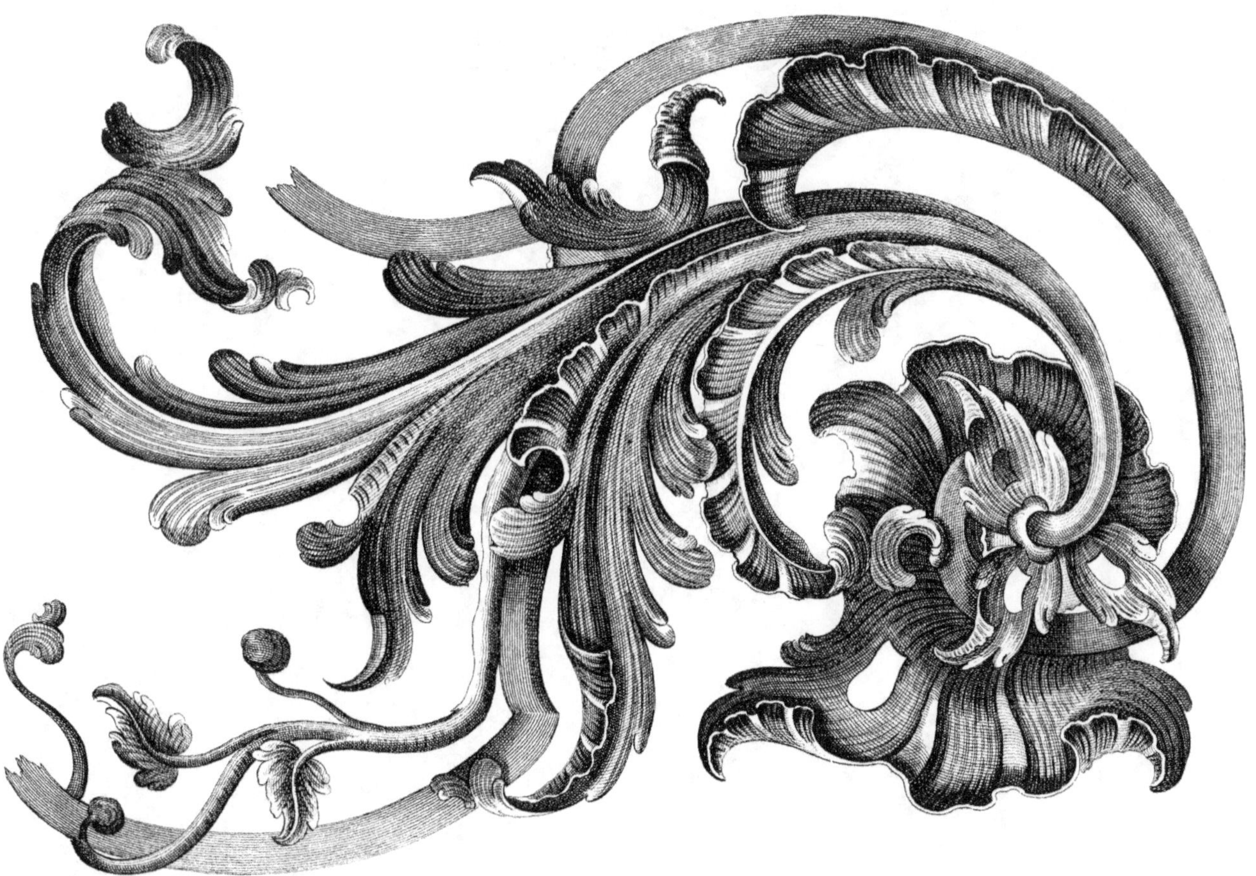

CUT & COLLAGE 3

GEMS, DIAMONDS & CRYSTALS

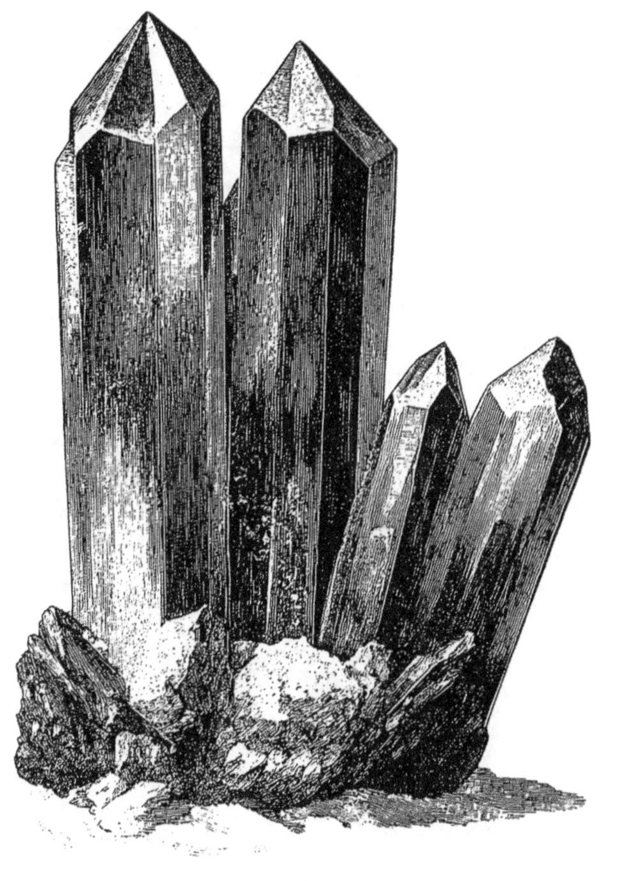
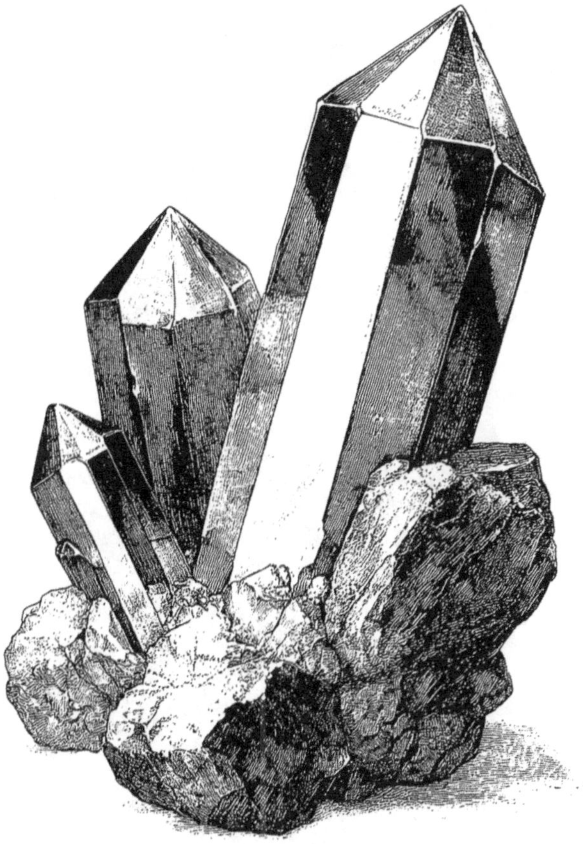
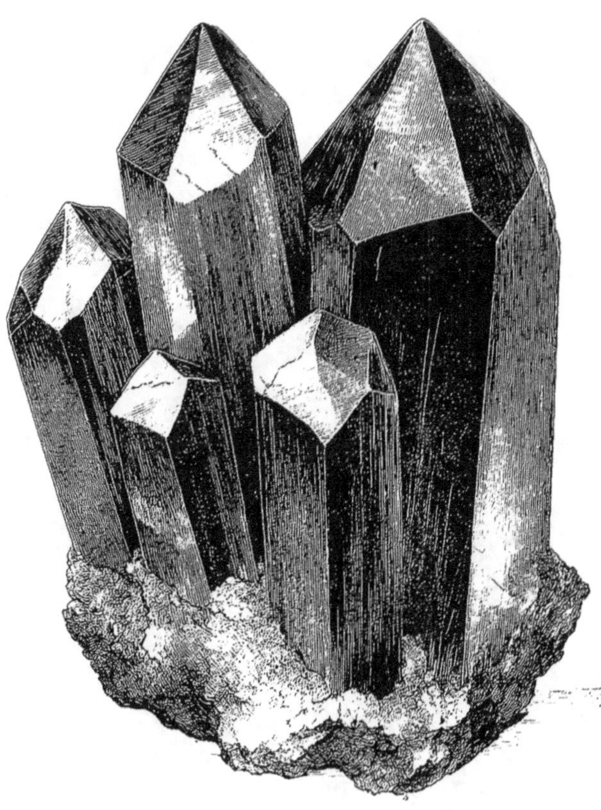
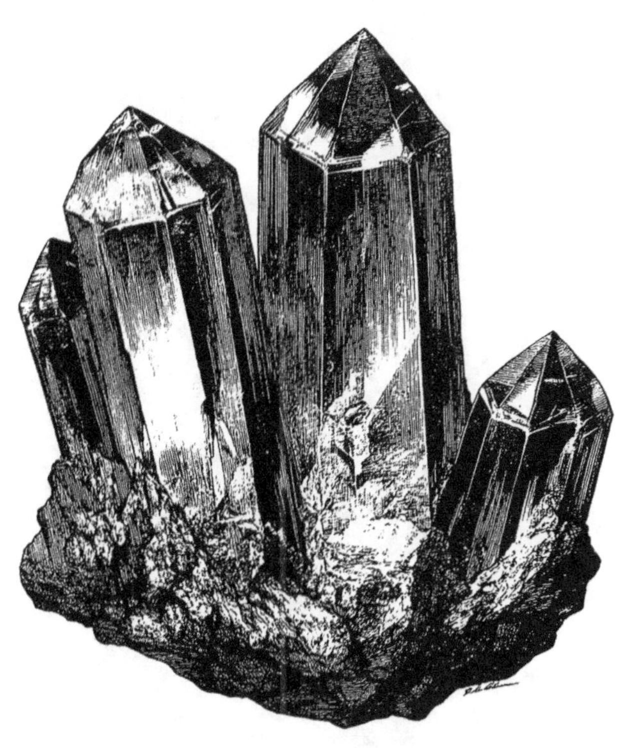

GEMS, DIAMONDS & CRYSTALS

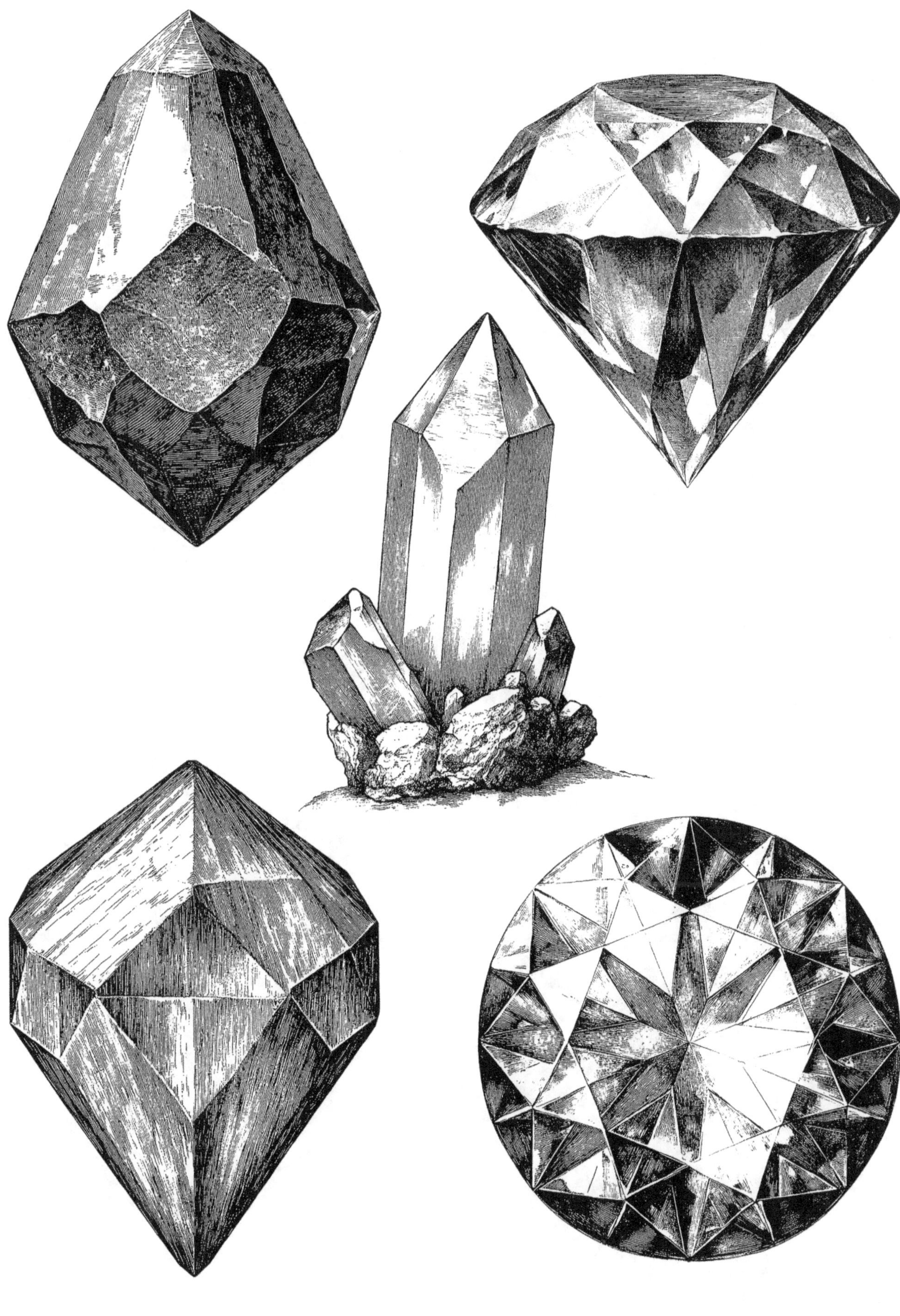

MEN

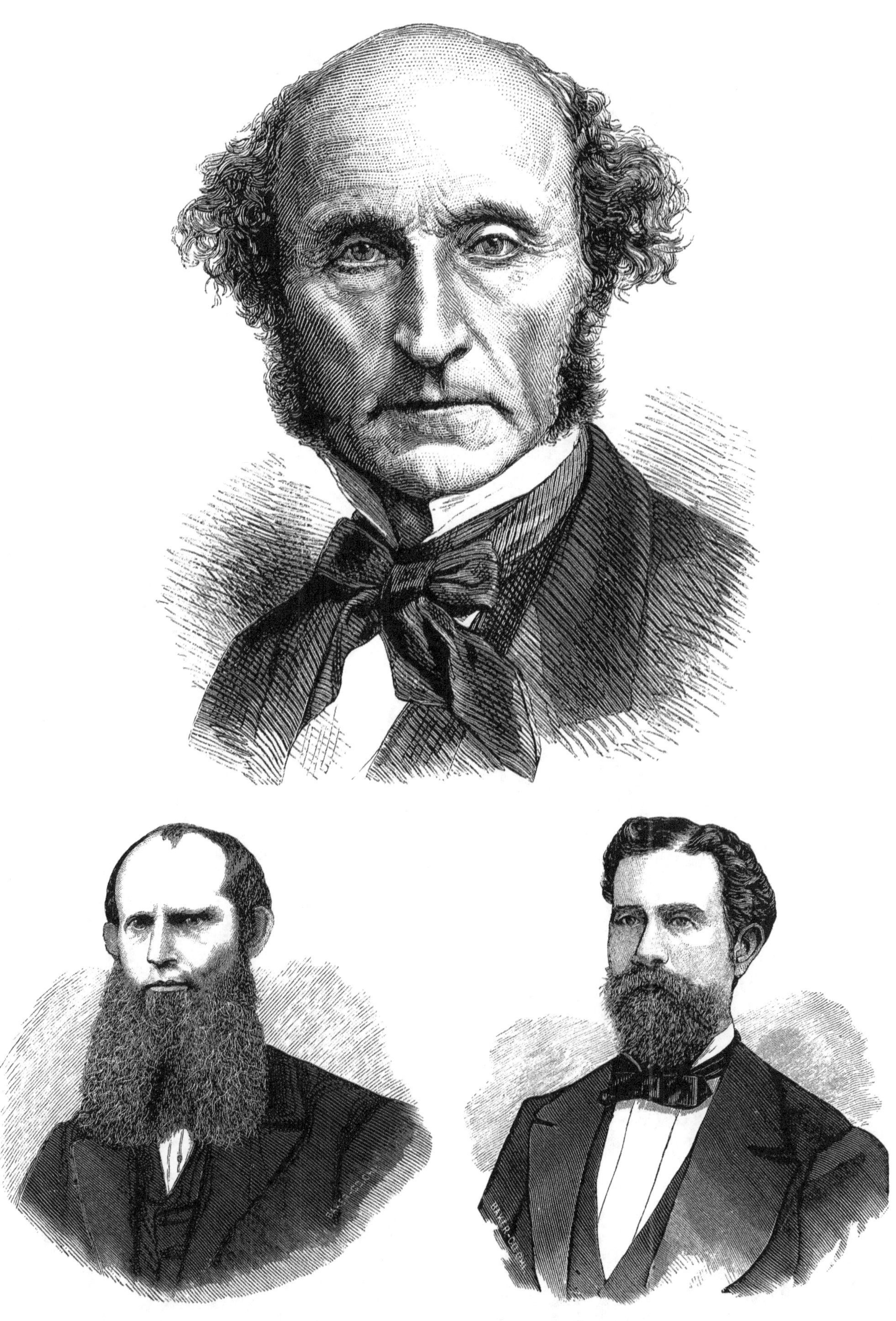

MEN

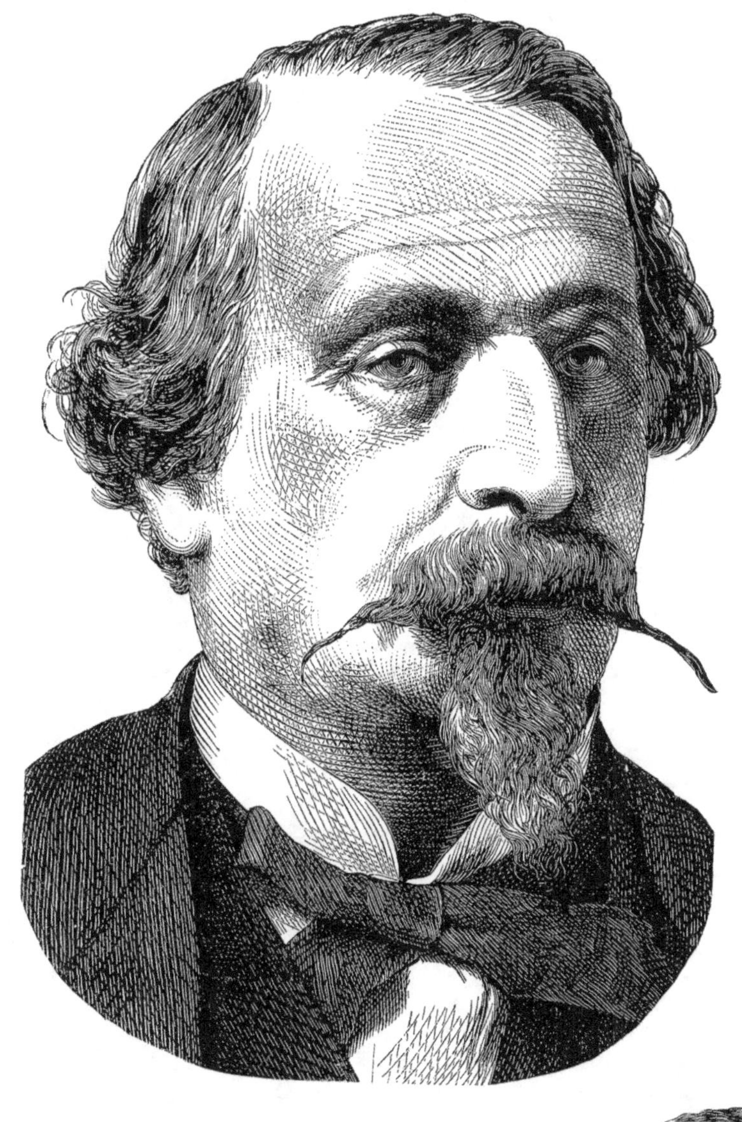

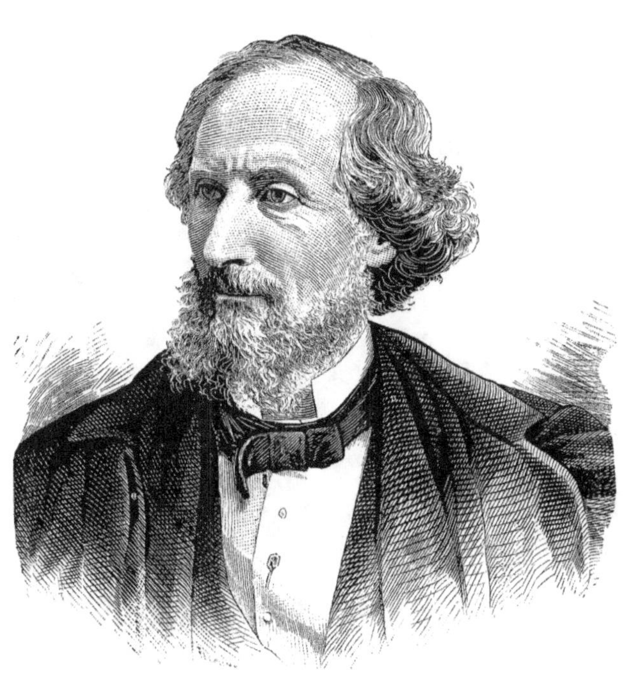

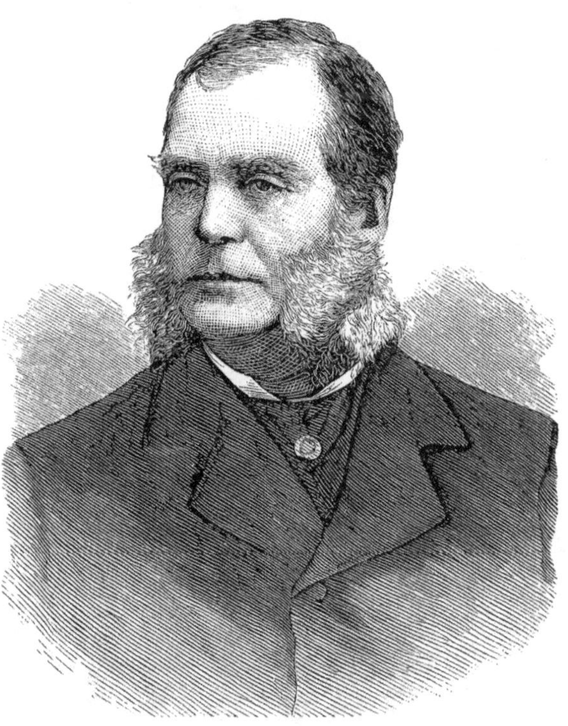

WOMEN

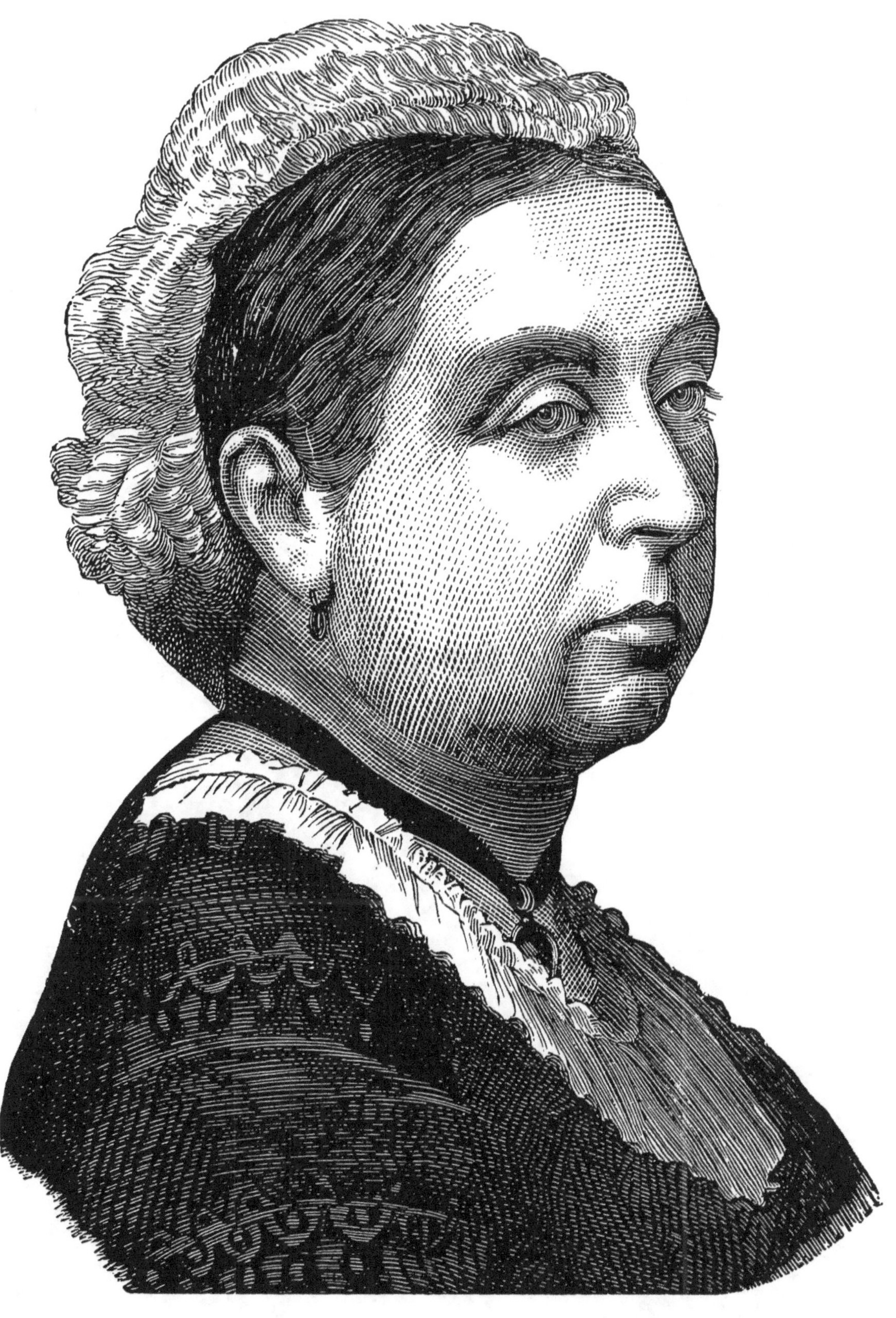

WOMEN

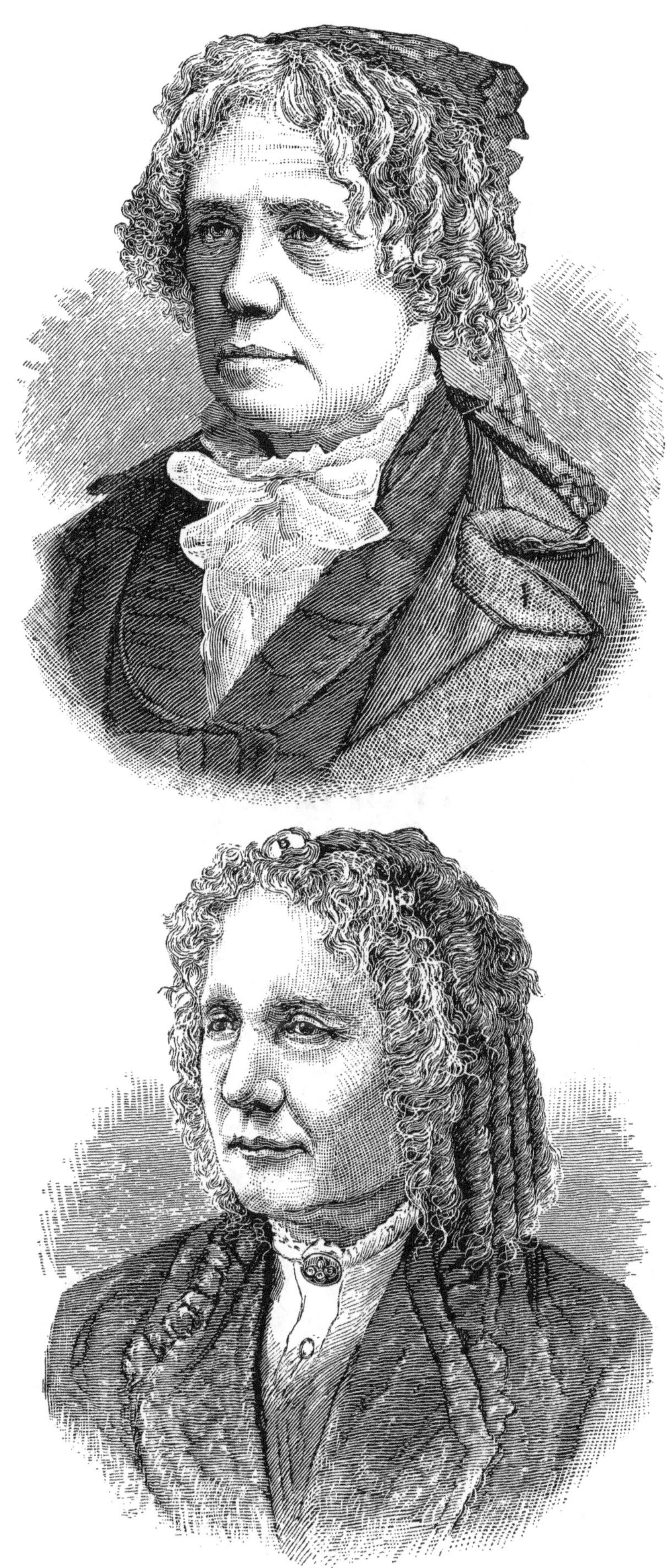

CUT&COLLAGE3

WOMEN

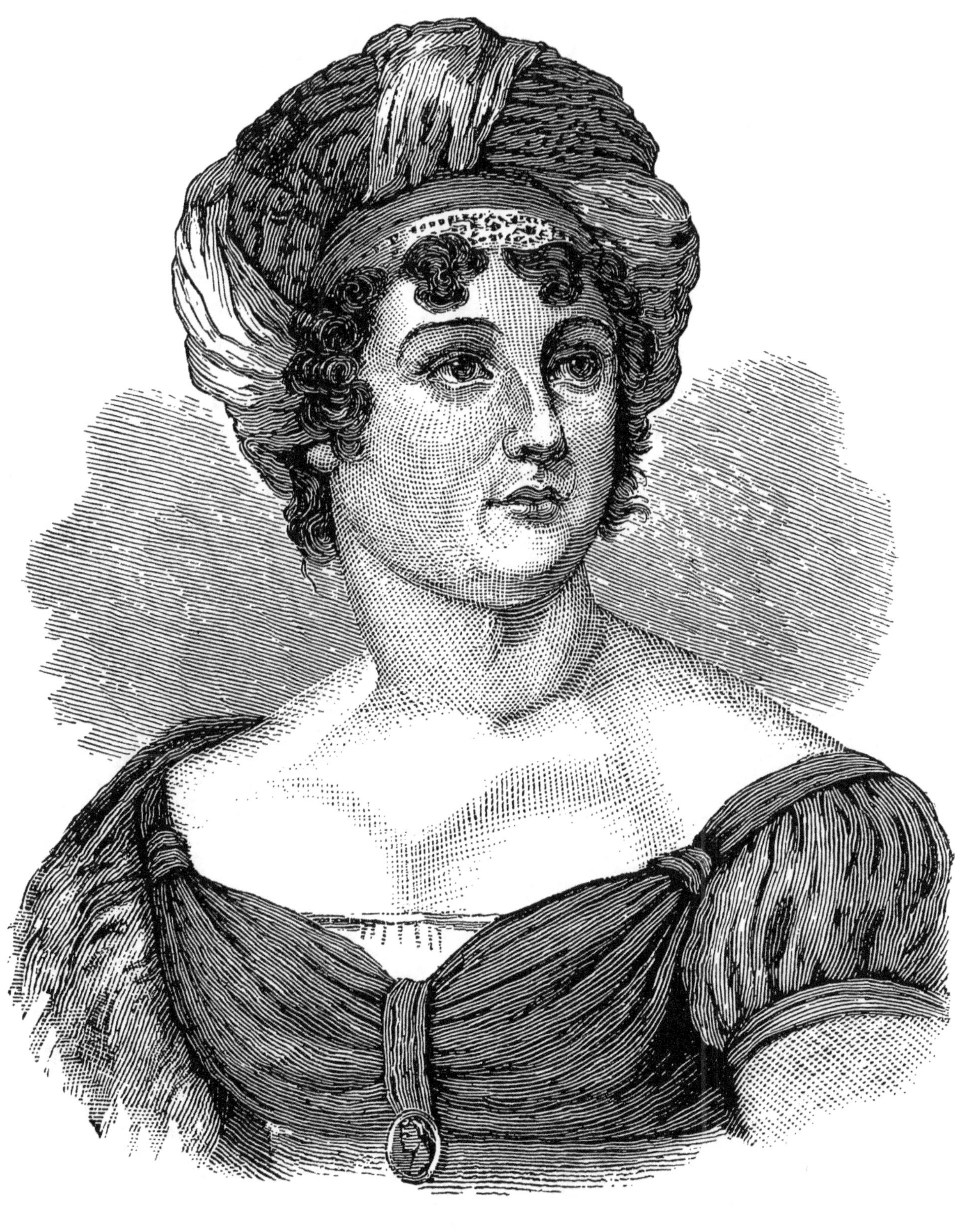

ARCHITECTURE

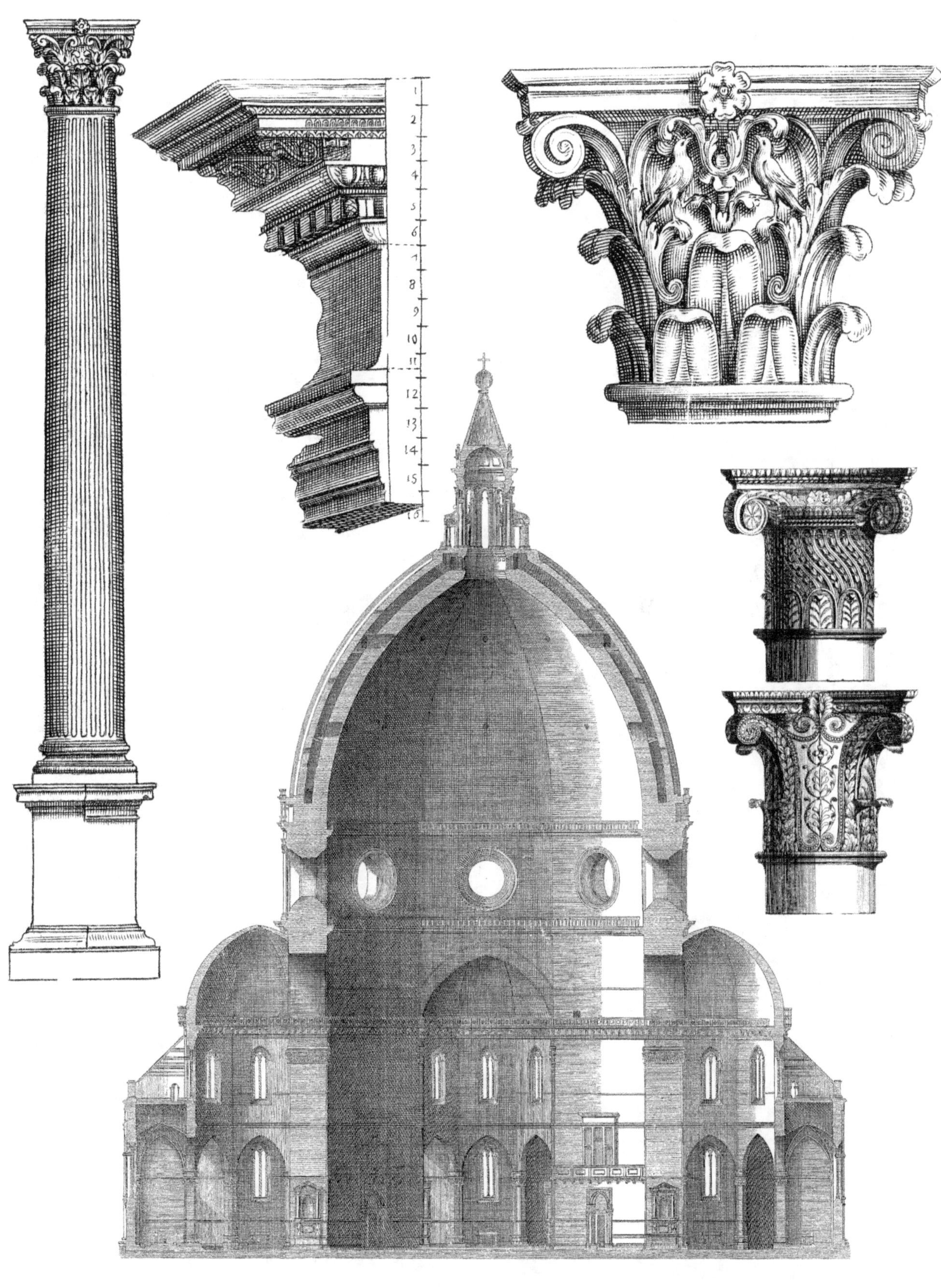

CUT & COLLAGE 3

ARCHITECTURE

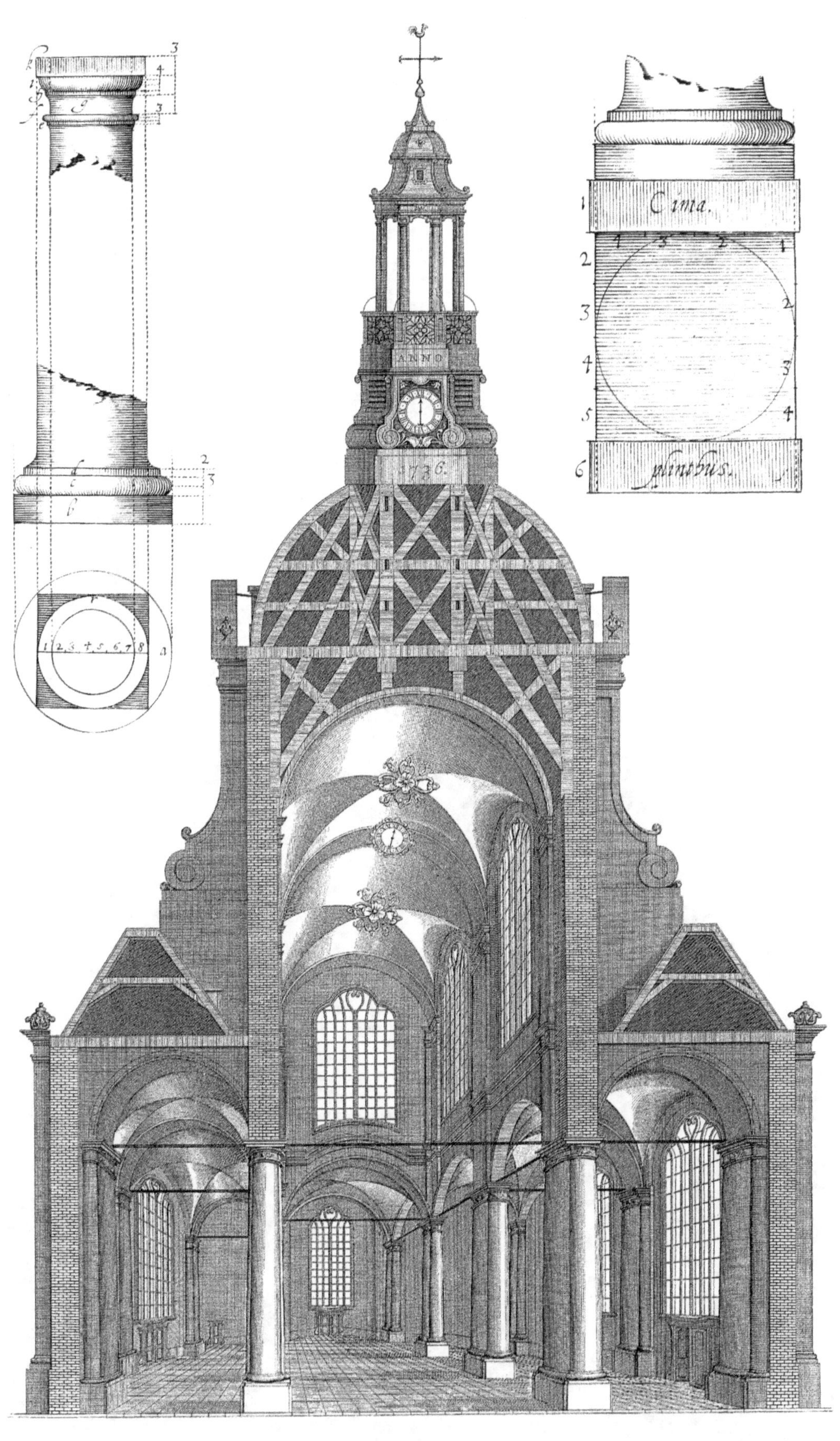
Cima.
ANNO
1736.
plintus.

ARCHITECTURE

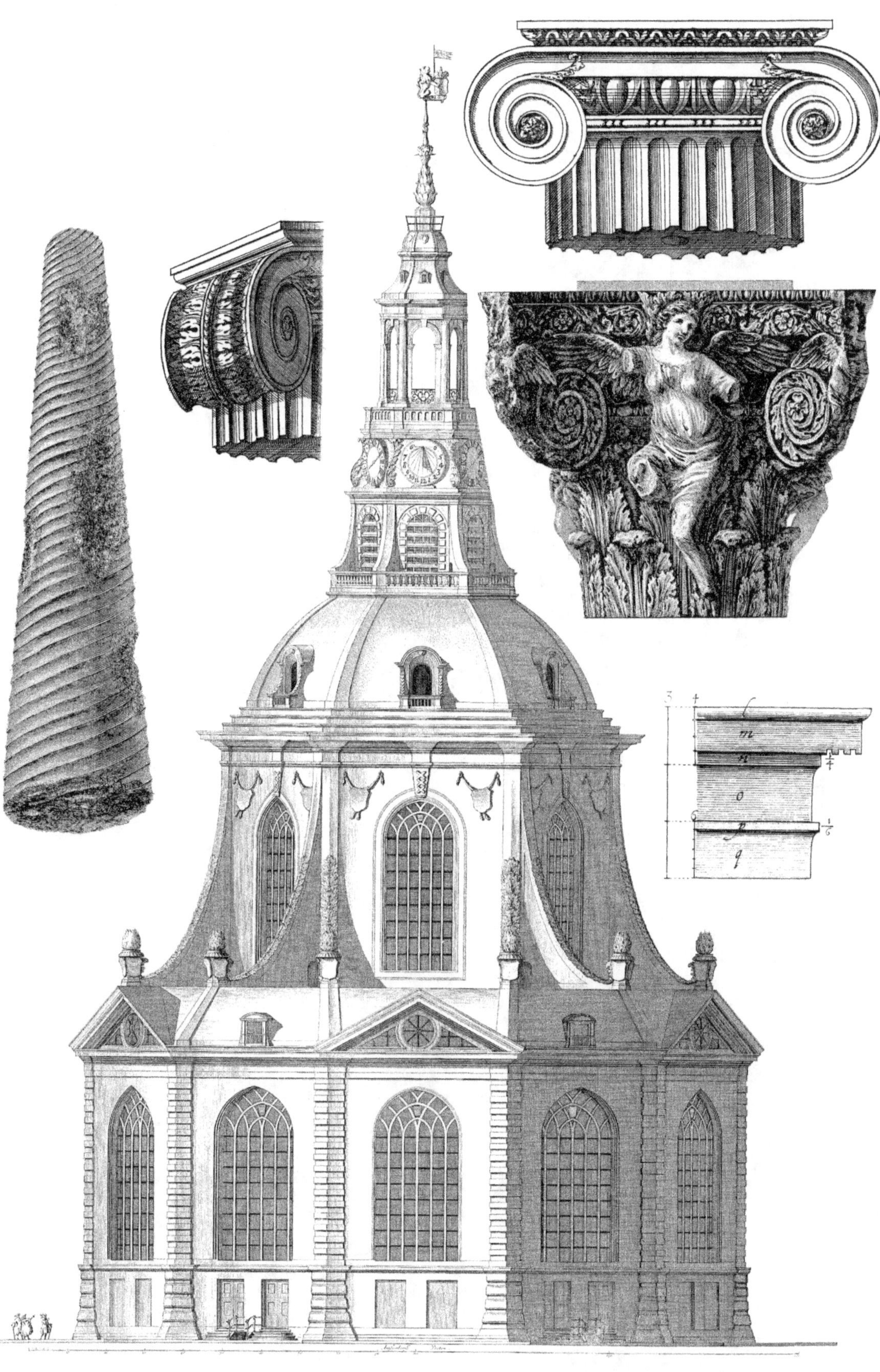

ARCHITECTURE

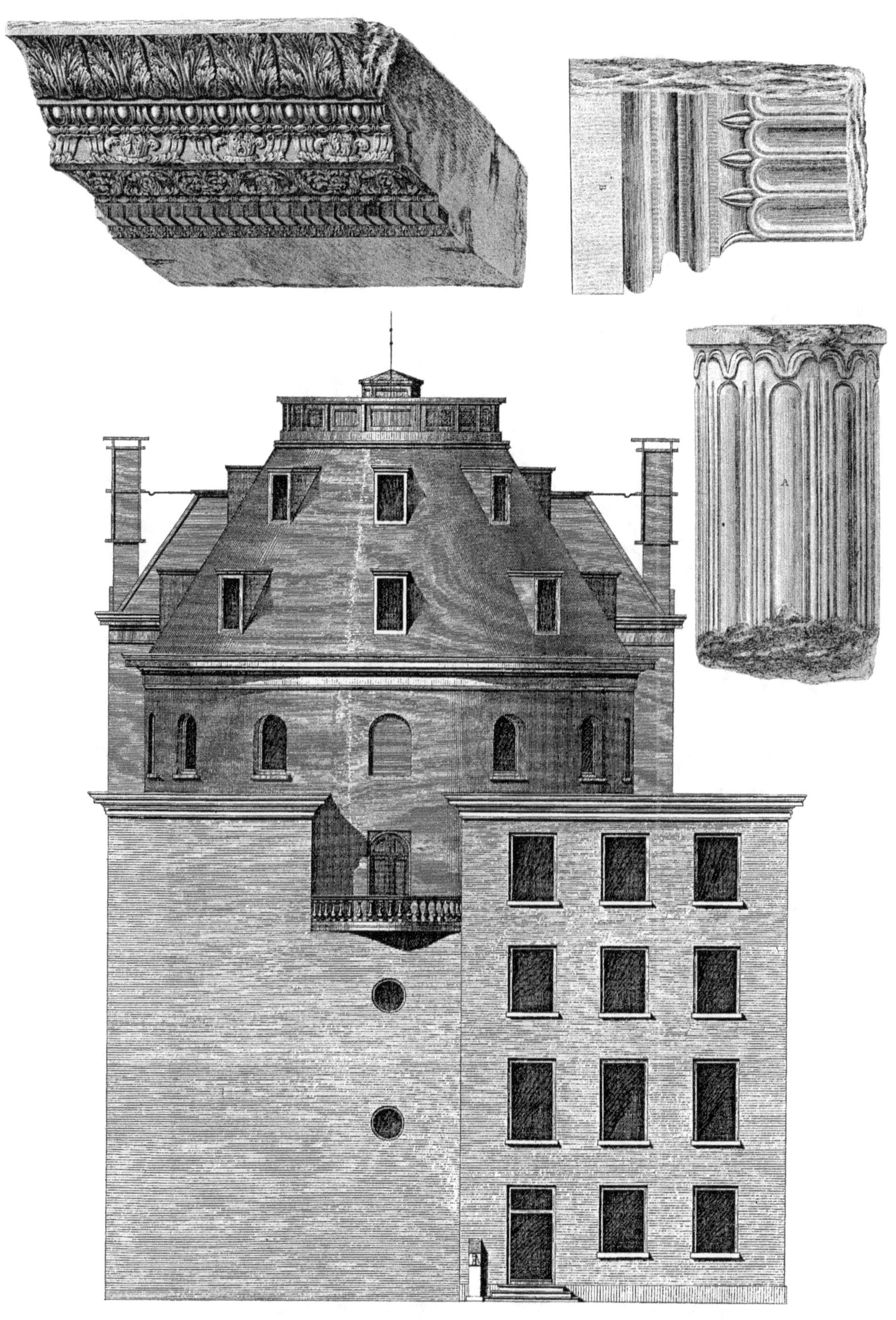

LANDSCAPES

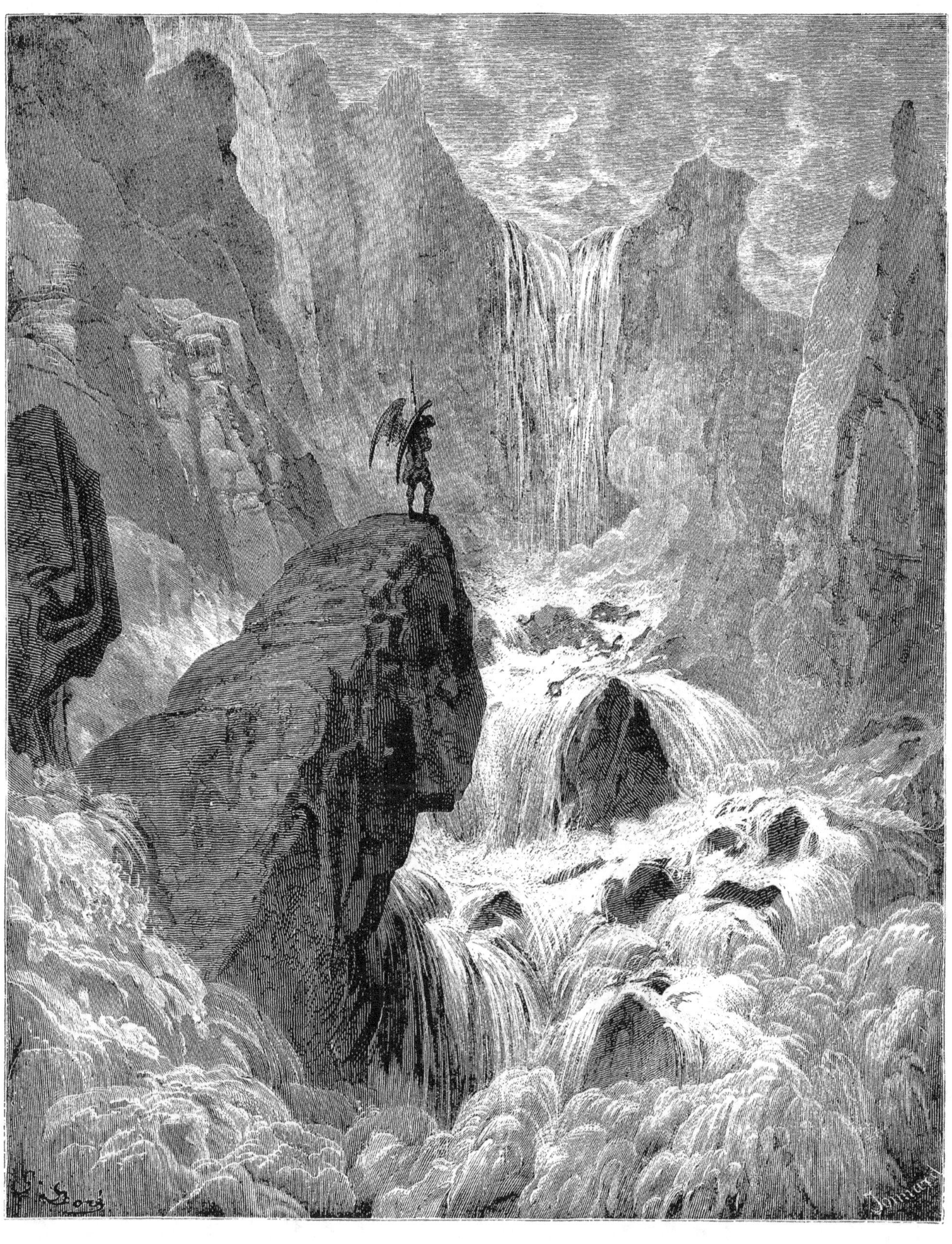

CUT & COLLAGE 3

LANDSCAPES

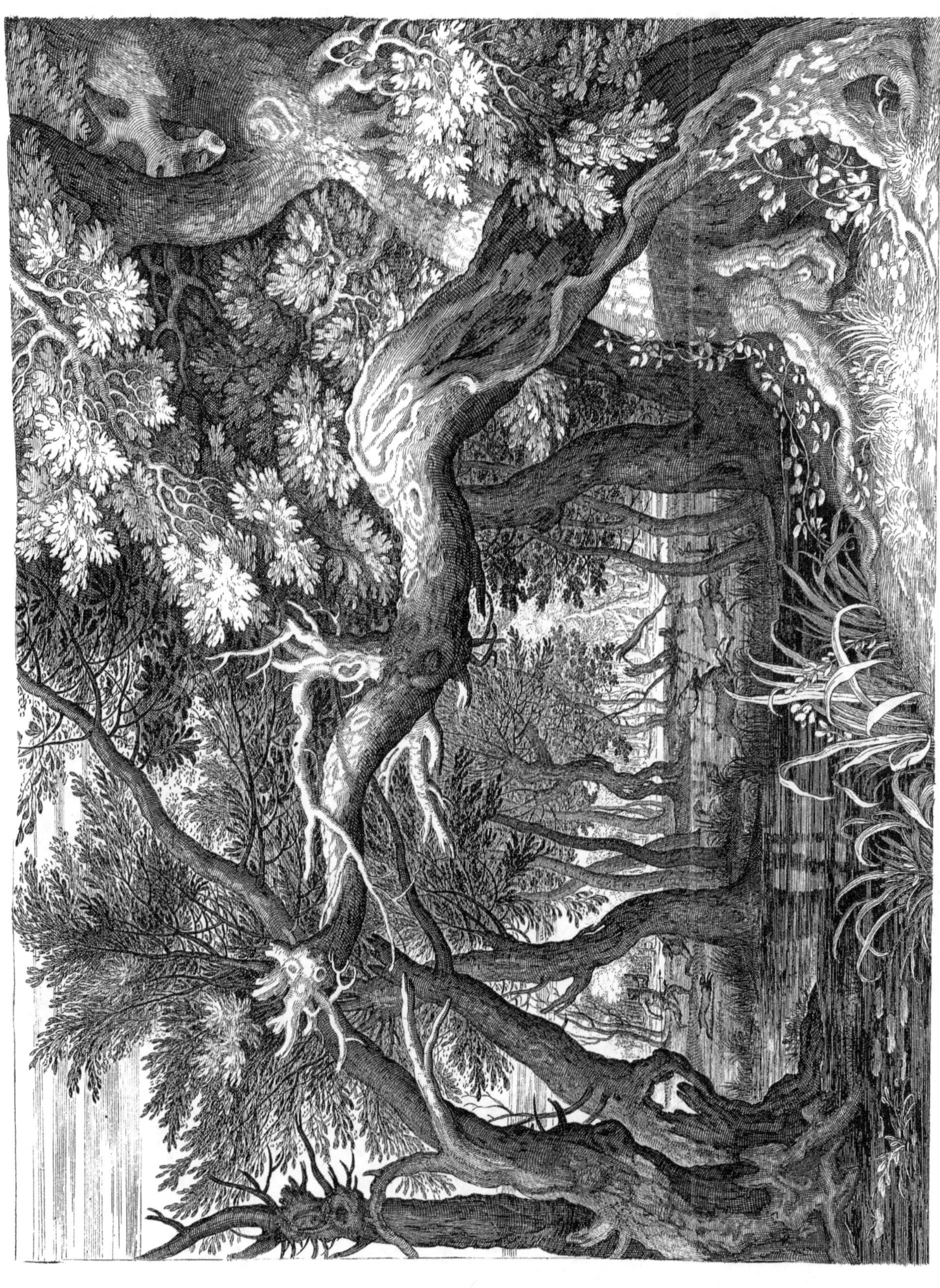

LANDSCAPES

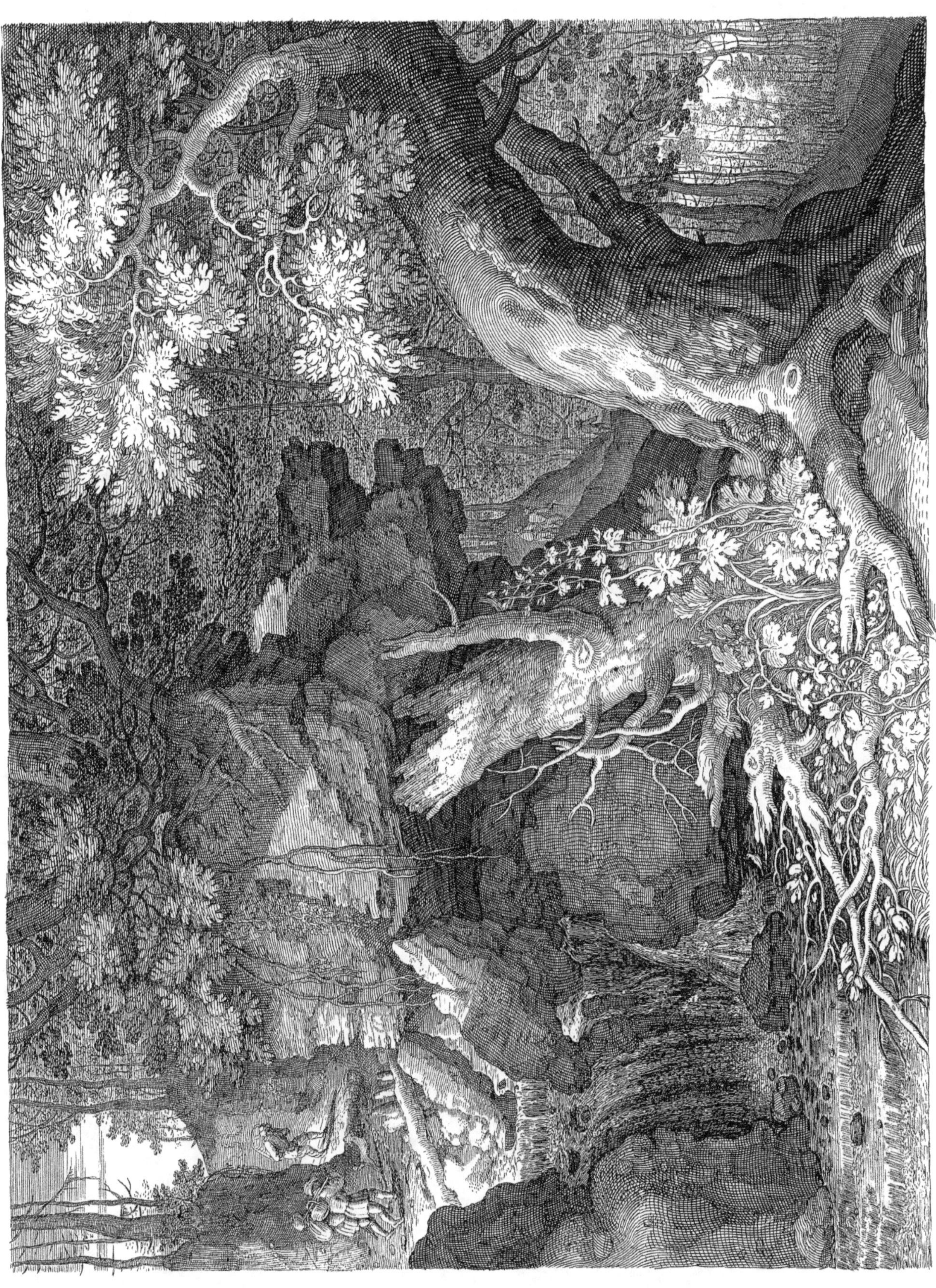

LANDSCAPES

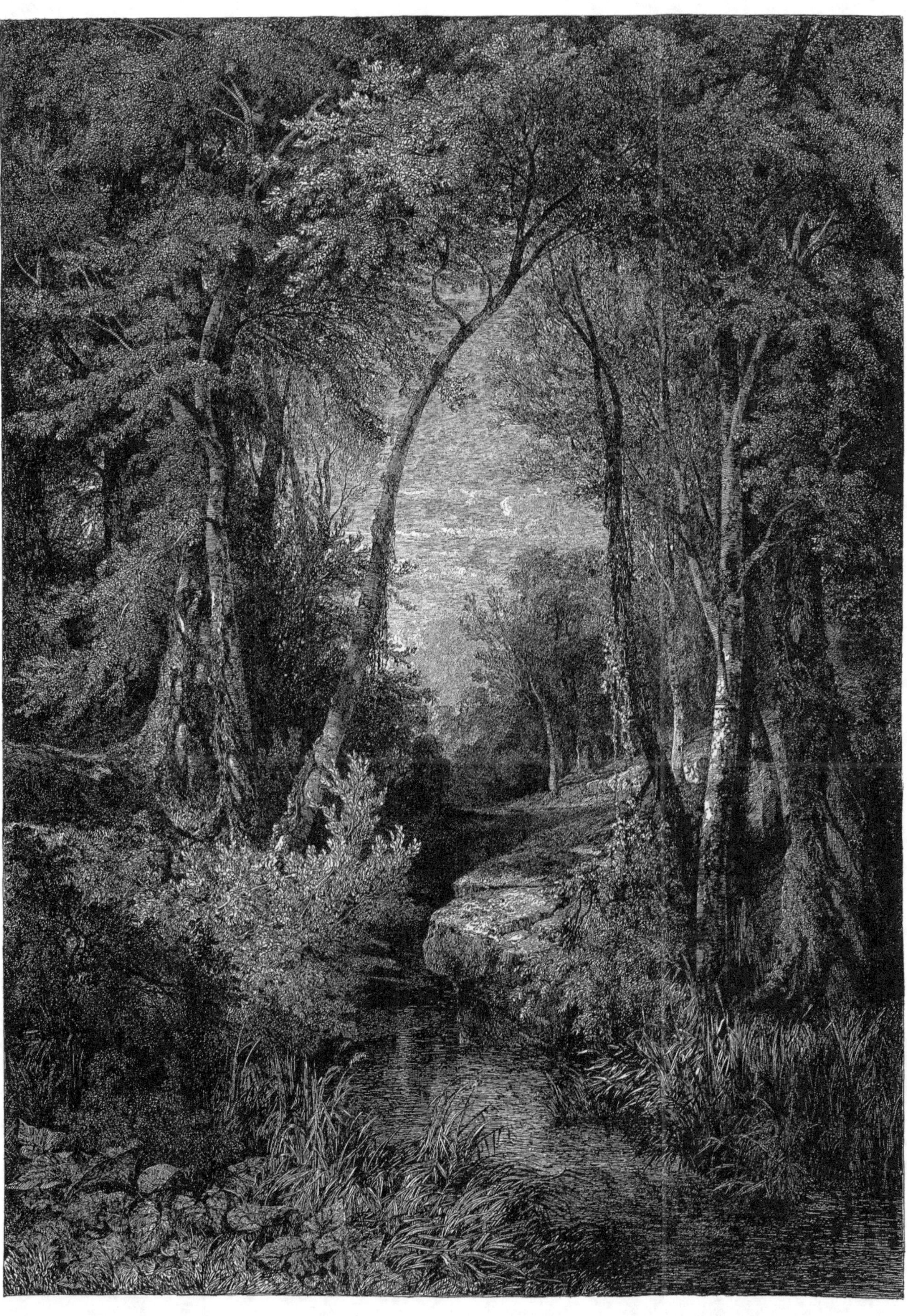

LANDSCAPES

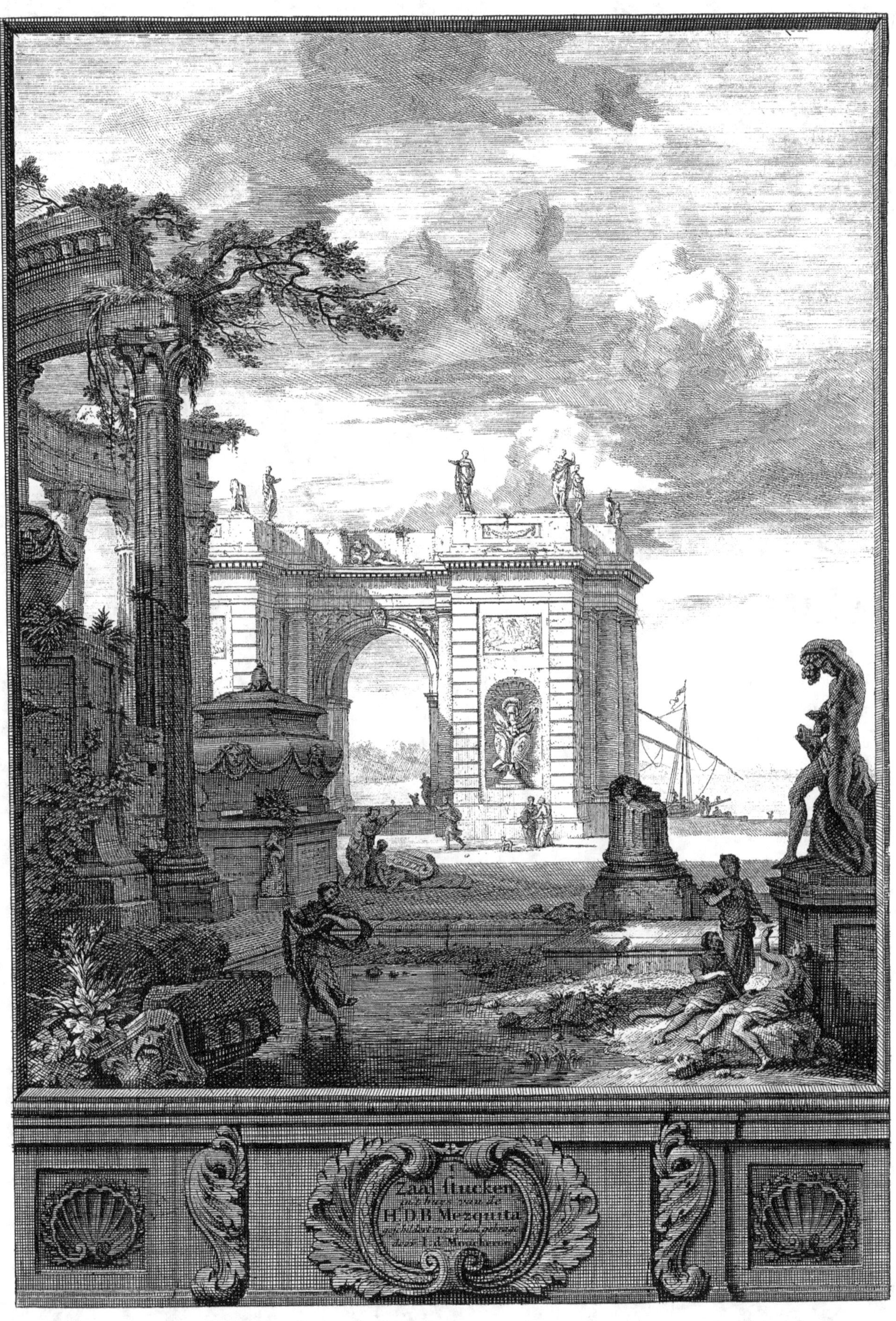
Zael stucken
H D B Mezquita

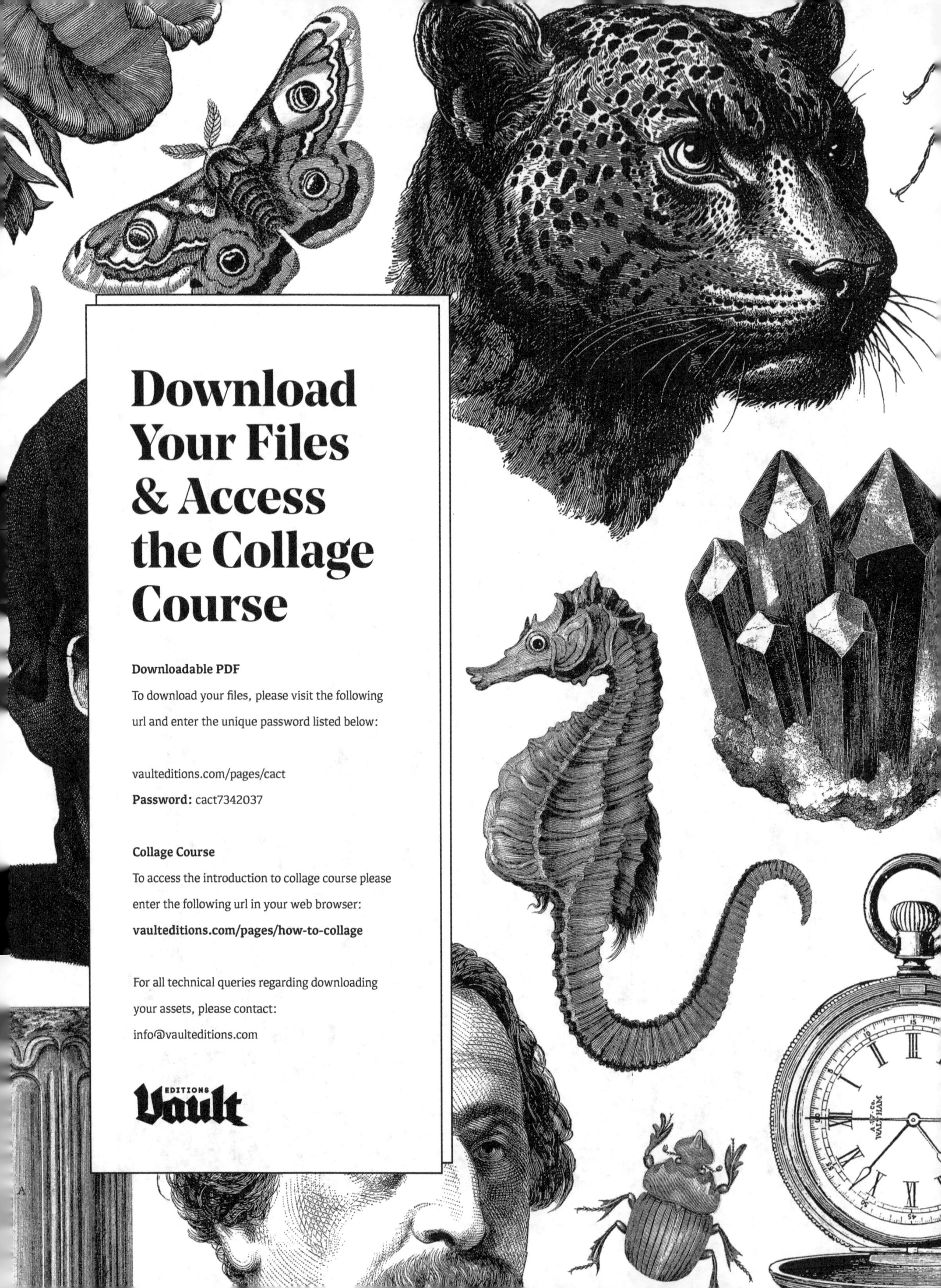

Download Your Files & Access the Collage Course

Downloadable PDF

To download your files, please visit the following url and enter the unique password listed below:

vaulteditions.com/pages/cact
Password: cact7342037

Collage Course

To access the introduction to collage course please enter the following url in your web browser:
vaulteditions.com/pages/how-to-collage

For all technical queries regarding downloading your assets, please contact:
info@vaulteditions.com

EDITIONS Vault